A More Expeditious Conveyance

*Monday next the experiment
for the more expeditious conveyance
of the mails will be made ... which
will be delivered in London
the next day.*
FARLEY'S BRISTOL JOURNAL
31st July, 1784

A More Expeditious Conveyance

The Story of the Royal Mail Coaches

Bevan Rider

J. A. Allen
London

British Library Cataloguing in Publication Data

Rider, Bevan
A more expeditious conveyance.
1. Postal service – Great Britain – History – 19th century.
2. Horse-drawn vehicles – Great Britain – History – 19th century.
I. Title
383'.143   HE6935

ISBN 0–85131–394–9

Published in Great Britain by
J. A. Allen & Company Limited,
1, Lower Grosvenor Place, Buckingham Palace Road,
London, SW1W 0EL

Book production Bill Ireson

Filmset VIP 11/12 Palatino by
Fakenham Photosetting Limited, Fakenham, Norfolk

Printed and bound by Butler & Tanner Limited,
Frome, Somerset

Dedicated to all those
who still carry the
Royal Mail

Contents

Contents

PART TWO *From St. Martin's le Grand*

Foreword

By Mr. John Richards, Past-Chairman and Vice-President of the British Driving Society

A More Expeditious Conveyance is a true chronicle of the great days of coaching. It mirrors and reflects the spirit of the men behind the Mail coach system which was the pride of Britain and the envy of the world. Running untaxed on the roads, they claimed the right of way over all other forms of transport and paid no tolls. To emphasise their rank the Royal cipher was picked out in gold on the foreboot and on each of the quarter panels were the Stars of the four Great Orders of Knighthood.

To name but one, the famous Quicksilver coach, the Devonshire Mail, became a legend in its time. Its name imparted the essence of its fame, speed and panache. It was the fastest long distance Mail in the country and had the unique distinction that it was the only Mail coach to carry a name.

With the passing of the Golden Age of Coaching, the leafy lanes and city pavements lost the sight, never to be repeated, of teams of high couraged horses put to the immaculately painted coaches. It was indeed a sight to wonder at and to savour.

The coaching revival was inspired by amateur coachmen who had travelled to their public schools by stagecoach and wished to recreate the excitement and adventure they remembered so well in their youth. Men such as Corbett, Lennox and Reynardson were able to set down their reminiscences which ensured that the true stories of the coach roads of England were not forgotten. The advent of the motor car was to have a profound effect and life was never to be the same again.

Bevan Rider has illuminated and highlighted the magic of the Golden Age and in this excellent book has encapsulated the true spirit of the age he so accurately portrays.

Acknowledgements

The author would like to thank the following for their assistance with the research of this book:

Mrs. J. Ferrugia, the archivist and her staff, General Post Office, St. Martin's-le-Grand.

Mr. Raife Wellsted, Curator, National Postal Museum.

The County Archivists of Devon, Dorset, Essex, Gloucestershire, Hampshire, Kent, Lincolnshire, Norfolk, Northamptonshire, Shropshire, Somerset, Sussex and Wiltshire.

The staff of record offices in almost every town mentioned in the book.

The Guildhall Library, London.

The libraries in the cities of Birmingham, Bristol, Edinburgh, Oxford, Newcastle-on-Tyne and York.

The Somerset Local History Library, Taunton, Somerset.

The librarian and staff of the Somerset Library, Bridgwater, Somerset for the considerable assistance they have given me.

Mr. H. V. Crees and Mr. M. G. Heenan, Canterbury, Kent.

Reverend E. Lane, the Vicar of Sixpenny Handley, Dorset.

Reverend G. H. Parsons, the Vicar of Burford, Gloucestershire.

Mr. R. Ricardo, Dorchester, Dorset.

Miss R. Rider, Plymouth, Devon.

Mrs. J. White, for research at Bangor, North Wales.

Mrs. R. Vincent, Oxford.

Mrs. J. Chynoweth, for painstakingly typing the manuscript.

My wife, who accompanied me, making notes on the many journeys undertaken.

Introduction

Whenever we drive today down any of the motorways or main roads in this country, how many of us give a thought to how our ancestors travelled a century and a half ago?

Time is losing its meaning as the whole world contracts and man continues to travel further and faster.

For thousands of years, until the coming of the railways, man had been limited by the speed and endurance of the horse. Since then new vistas have been opened up, new horizons reached, but in saving time we have lost part of the enjoyment of travel, time to view the countryside through which one is passing. Travel by coach for all its drawbacks and discomforts enabled one to achieve this pleasure. By car, however, there is only time to glimpse.

Few travelled by coach in the early part of the 18th century, and those that did had to accept unbelievable hardships by our standards. The roads were bad, the coaches were slow, clumsy and uncomfortable and journeys were restricted to daylight hours in the summer only. In the 1750s a coach travelling from Manchester to London, a distance of 190 miles, was advertised as taking four-and-a-half days. Highwaymen were common, and prudent travellers made their wills before undertaking such a journey.

In the diary of Sylas Neville, dated 1771, a journey is recorded on the London to Newcastle stagecoach from Stilton to Newcastle. To cover the 197 miles it took two days travelling day and night at a speed of about four miles per hour.

Ordinary folk in those times just ventured as far as their horses or feet could carry them in one day. Gradually, with the increase of both Mail and stagecoaches both on the main routes and bye-roads (cross-country routes), more innkeepers kept post-horses. In 1512 the office of "Master of the Posts" had been created, and Sir Brian Tuke was authorised "to maintain posts to Berwick and Calais and elsewhere as required."

Originally certain innkeepers were ordered to keep horses in readiness for the King's Messengers, but by the 17th century horses were kept for those who wished to travel by post-chaise. The expression "travelling by post" was used, which had nothing to do with the post-boys who carried the Royal Mail, although they also changed horses at these inns.

In the middle 1760s it was realised that the roads must be improved and this led to the creation of many more Turnpike Trusts, set up by Acts of Parliament. The trustees were authorised to carry out the improvements necessary and allowed to levy tolls. Tolls were very unpopular, and there were many instances of pulling down the turnpike gates. The gatekeepers, referred to as "Pykie", were subject to constant abuse from all classes of society, and often robbed and sometimes murdered in the course of their duty. Better roads resulted from the Turnpike system and traffic increased to use them, but it was the work of engineers Telford and MacAdam that made possible the standards achieved by the stagecoach and Mail coaches in the period 1820 to 1840.

By 1780 the postal service had deteriorated to such an extent that a post-chaise hired privately, and some of the faster coaches, covered the distance from Bath to London in between sixteen to eighteen hours whereas the Mail, carried by post-boys on horseback, took up to forty hours for the same journey. Alone, unarmed, and often carrying mail containing valuables the post-boys were subjected to frequent robberies, but such was the complacency of the Post Office that all they did about the matter was to advise senders of banknotes to cut them in half and send each half by a separate post.

At this time a gentleman by the name of John Palmer was the manager of the Theatres Royal in Bath and Bristol, and had access to a number of influential people including William Pitt. Palmer, like many others, felt that reform of the Post Office service was long overdue, it having carried on unchanged since 1603 when set up by royal decree. He might well have been inspired by Ralph Allen's success in developing the cross-post system earlier in the century. Palmer's plan was simple. Instead of the present slow and unsafe method of carrying mail, which he referred to as "the idle boys without Character, mounted on a worn-out Hack, who, so far from being able to defend himself or escape from a Robber is more likely to be in league with him" the mails would be conveyed by special coach. This coach would be contracted to carry the mail and a guard to protect it at the same rate of 3d. a mile paid for the post-boy and horse. Palmer anticipated that the coach would maintain a speed of eight miles per hour, including stops, night and day in all weathers (excepting fog and snow), and it should pay no tolls. The strict punctuality of the "Mail Machine" as he termed it, would be a further safeguard, as non-arrival at each stage at the appointed time would be a cause for enquiry. He suggested ex-soldiers as the most suitable persons for the service of guards, as they were used to the handling of firearms, and also to "the watch and fatigue of Late Hours".

Although Palmer's plan met with Mr. Pitt's approval it was not until 31st July, 1784, that *Farley's Bristol Journal* was able to announce:

Monday next the experiment for the most expeditious conveyance of the mails will be made on the road from London to Bath and Bristol: the letters to be put into the London Office every evening before eight, and to arrive next morning at Bath by ten, and at Bristol at twelve o'clock (noon) – the letters for London, or any place between or beyond, to be put into the Bristol Office before three, and into the Bath Office every evening before six o'clock; which will be delivered in London the next day.

The first Mail coach left the Rummer Tavern at four o'clock on the afternoon of 2nd August, 1784, and according to contemporary newspapers arrived in London at the Swan with Two Necks well before eight o'clock the following morning. It had travelled 119 miles in under sixteen hours. The coach which left London at eight in the evening arrived in Bristol before noon the following day.

Palmer was right, the impact on the public was astounding, on the bureaucrats of the Post Office one of complete opposition. They even compiled a record of their criticism which ran to three volumes in perfect copperplate writing. However, the trial which was originally for nine days was extended, and by the following year coaches were running to Norwich, Liverpool, Leeds, Dover and Exeter.

It is interesting to note how this very efficient organisation was run. Jobmasters, or coachmasters, undertook under contract to provide horses at each stage, usually about ten miles, and they also provided the coachman. Special coaches were built by Besant to his patent design, and after his death in 1791 his partner John Vidler continued the business. The original design was so good it changed very little over fifty years.

The coaches were hired on a mileage basis by the Post Office, who appointed suitable employees as guards, and gave them a uniform of scarlet livery. These men had to be able to read and write to be able to complete the timesheet (also referred to as the Way-bill) and they carried a timepiece set each evening before they left the General Post Office. Each guard was given training at Vidlers yard in how to cope with simple breakdowns, and they carried on the coach a set of tools for such occasions.

In 1815 a Post Office directive laid down precise *Instructions to Guards*, and at that time only two passengers were allowed on the outside, one on the box, the other on the seat behind the box. Furthermore the guard was:

> ... not to quit or desert the Mail, or suffer any loitering or stopping at public houses.

Guards were liable to be dismissed, suspended, or fined if they failed to deliver the letter bags properly, and they must remain sealed. Great stress was laid on keeping the box containing the mail bags locked at all times. The directive again:

Drunkenness or disobedience of official orders will disqualify them for serving as Mail Guards upon any road in the Kingdom.

There were instructions concerning the sounding of the horn – to clear the way, warn the keepers of the turnpike gates, alert the postmasters, and horsekeepers of the approach of the Mail. They were not allowed to use a key bugle which the guards on later stagecoaches used to great effect to keep the passengers amused and also in the hope of a larger tip.

The most unpopular of all the Mail guard's duties was to report any misdemeanour on the part of the coachman employed by the contractors.

In cases where, due to floods or snow or a serious breakdown, the coach was unable to proceed the guard was to go forward on horseback – never mind the passengers – their fares went to the contractors!

The guards were paid half a guinea a week plus sick pay and a pension.

It appears from the records available that Mr. Hasker, the Chief Superintendent of Mail from 1792 until 1817, was fairly lenient on the guards for what might be termed minor offences, allowing them to carry personal goods in moderation, and to make arrangements with local newspapers, always provided that it did not interfere with the coach being run on time. Tips were allowed, and in the days when the mails carried seven passengers, after about 1815, a full coach could mean tips would be around 14s. a journey.

The following notice to guards is evidence enough of the penalties for more serious crimes:

Gentlemen,

I am very sorry to order in all the Guards to witness a dismissal of one old in the Service but so imperious is the duty that was he my Brother he must be dismissed. Indeed I do not think there is a Guard who hears this but will say a man who goes into an Alehouse stays to drink (and at Brentford) at the dusk of the Morning leaving his Mail box unlocked Deserves to lose his situation. And he is dismissed accordingly. And I am sure I need not tell you to avoid such misconduct – to read your instructions and mind them. I am the more Sorry for this as guards – who have been some time in the Service are fit for no other duty.

T. Hasker.

The coaching organisation was built up and maintained by a small number of proprietors. William Chaplin, Benjamin Horne, Edward Sherman, Robert Nelson and Robert Fagg were the men who operated the principal coaching establishments in London. Working with them were a considerable number of smaller contractors or jobmasters all over the country responsible for supplying teams of horses at each stage on the road. Including "horsing the mails" these five gentlemen put on the road their own stagecoaches, which by the 1830s meant they and their organisations were responsible for over 250 coaches leaving London each day.

In the Post Office records is a *Return of Mail Coaches in England* dated June, 1835. It reveals that there were at that time twenty-eight mails leaving London each night, and seventy-five provincial coaches travelling between places such as Birmingham to Liverpool, Derby to Manchester, Pontefract to Leeds and so on. At the same time over each route a coach was travelling in the reverse direction, those working up to London arriving at the General Post Office at various times between five-thirty and seven in the morning. Approximately these 206 coaches covered about 15,000 miles each twenty-four hours.

Although passengers commencing their journeys in London could assemble at various advertised coaching establishments, they would then have to proceed to Lombard Street, the headquarters of the Post Office until 1829 when it moved to St. Martins le Grand. All the Mail coaches travelling from London left at eight o'clock in the evening, but to ease the congestion the six Western Mails departed from the Gloucester Coffee House in Piccadilly half an hour later. This number was increased in 1835 to seven with the addition of a direct Mail coach to Stroud.

To travel with the Mail necessitated a night journey, and it cost about 1d. per mile more than a stagecoach, but there was the reassurance of the armed guard. The coachmen were reliable drivers, also referred to as "whips", the vehicle was the best on the road, and the timekeeping very dependable. Moreover there was the prestige of the Royal Mail itself.

Author's Note

Between 1825 and 1838 remarkable changes were made in the timing of the Mails, and such improvements often resulted in alterations to the stops made for a change of horses. As the Mails used the nearest inn or coaching office adjacent to the post office in the town through which they passed, any alteration in the site of the post office could result in the choice of a different inn for the change. For this reason the times of the Mails and the posting inns mentioned in Part One are all taken from sources published between 1825 and 1830. Those in Part Two from material published around 1835 to 1838.

As many of the inns referred to in the text no longer exist careful drawings have been made from prints published at the time.

The spelling of certain villages and towns differs slightly from today because they have been quoted as they appear in the road guides of the time. Also the distances recorded are from the same sources.

PART ONE

From Hyde Park Corner

1 The Devonport Mail (Quicksilver)

Travelling by way of Salisbury and Shaftesbury

On fine summer evenings in London considerable crowds would gather in Piccadilly to observe the departure of the Western Mails. Assembled at the Gloucester Coffee House, where the Berkeley Hotel now stands, would be six coaches all painted the same. The sides of the front of the coach were black and so too were those of the back boot which bore its number. The panels of the lower part of the bodywork were maroon and the door carried the insignia of the Royal Arms, the words "Royal Mail" and the names of the two towns between which the coach travelled. The upper bodywork of the coach was black with the Stars of the Garter and Thistle on the nearside and the Bath and St. Patrick on the offside. The undercarriage and wheels were painted scarlet.

These coaches had arrived in Piccadilly with passengers who had assembled at the Spread Eagle and at the Swan with Two Necks in Lad Lane, the Bell and Crown at Holborn or the Golden Cross, Charing Cross. The mails themselves were brought in vans from the General Post Office in Lombard Street. All had to be ready by half-past eight.

Coachmen checked the teams with the ostlers. These teams were the best of bloodstock, provided by men such as William Chaplin, Benjamin Horne and Robert Fagg who horsed the first stage out of town and took a great pride in the quality of horse provided. Guards, appointed to be custodians of His Majesty's mails, resplendent in their scarlet livery, checked their firearms, the passenger list and the loading of the mail. Those engaged in this nightly operation knew it was regarded as a spectacle and were quite capable of playing to the gallery. Coachmen took their seats with dignity, adjusted their aprons with care and, taking up their whips, ordered the ostlers to remove the horse cloths. A glance back to the guard who then looked at his timepiece. When the appointed time was almost reached, he would call out "All ready inside and out", and then at exactly half past eight they were off. The crowd cheered – they adored the excitement and colour of the occasion as the six coaches trotted smartly towards Hyde Park Corner.

Custom decreed that the Bristol coach, running over this, the oldest established Royal Mail route, led the procession towards Hyde Park Corner and, with the exception of the Devonport coach, Quicksilver, the others would still be together when they reached Hounslow.

18

At this time, between 1825 and 1830, the average speed of the Western Mails was just over eight miles an hour, but Quicksilver's schedule meant an average of well over nine miles an hour to reach Devonport in twenty-four hours. It was a crack coach with jobmasters having to provide excellent horses. It was also the only Mail coach to be given a name. Doubtless coachmen were proud to drive this vehicle and the guards would be able to carry the news for no-one could carry it faster. They had unofficial arrangements with local newspaper offices for modest returns which helped to augment their pay.

In 1825 the old turnpike gate at Hyde Park Corner was moved to a position west of the corner itself and in its place the fine triple gates to the park, based on designs by Decimus Burton, were erected the following year.

On the north side of Hyde Park Corner is Apsley House, given to the Duke of Wellington by a grateful nation after Waterloo. The red brick mansion, its address is No.1 London, was originally built in 1785 for Lord Apsley, Chancellor Bathurst. When the Bathurst family commenced building on the site they could hardly have been expected to know that, about forty years previously, George II, when walking in the park, had spoken to a soldier who had fought with him at Dettingen. This man, called Allen, begged the king to give him the grant of a small parcel of land on which for some time past he had erected his stall. His request was granted. Later the stall became a cottage known as "Allen's Stall", where apprentice lads from the City took their girls when on a visit to the park. Eventually, after the death of both Allen and his wife, the cottage became derelict and was later demolished. Allen's son was an attorney, and he waited until the Bathurst family had almost completed building before pressing his claim to a part of their site. His rights were finally agreed at a ground rent of £450 per annum!

The coaches left the stones of the London roads past St. George's Hospital, and passed unhindered through the Knightsbridge turnpike gate. With six coaches passing through at once, the gatekeepers would have opened both gates. The village of Knightsbridge consisted of one long street of rather shabby properties which backed on to the north side of the Park itself. In those days the Westbourne stream was a constant source of flooding with the result that the state of the road was appalling and the cause of much complaint. One of the semi-derelict properties adjoining the road was the Cannon Brewery, later demolished for the erection of the Albert Gate, and further on, on the same side of the road, was Knightsbridge Barracks, erected in 1795 and pulled down in 1878. There was accommodation in these barracks for 600 men and 500 horses. Prior to the 1851 Great Exhibition, a number of the older buildings on the north side of the road were taken down.

It is difficult now to think of Kensington as the village it was in the 1820s. Near the road the coaches took was Kensington Palace, the home of Queen Victoria in her childhood, and indeed it had been a popular royal residence since Sir Christopher Wren converted it for King William III.

In complete contrast to the palace was another well-known landmark, a squalid set of buildings known as the Half-way House. For a long time there had been suggestions to the effect that it should be demolished and not only on account of the state of the property. Its very history was one of crime and violence. Here in 1740 the Bristol Mail was robbed; here William Belchier, a notorious highwayman, was caught some ten years later. At this point more than one highwayman had been hanged and from here dozens of petty crooks, footpads and robbers had conducted their daily business. From here also informers were able to obtain all the information they required concerning the coaches and occupants travelling in and out of town. The Half-way House was demolished in 1846.

Beyond Kensington the coaches followed a country road until Hammersmith was reached. Just past a turning to Brook Gardens there stood a fine old hostelry called the Red Cow. It was built some time in the 16th century and behind its rather unpretentious frontage, with its high pitched red tiled roof, were vast stables. In the early 1800s this was the first stage out of town and consequently the stable yard was busy day and night. Here were kept a good supply of strong horses for coaches running to Bath, Bristol, Exeter (both routes), Gloucester and Poole. Here those elegant "town creatures" which had hauled the coach from the Spread Eagle, the Swan with Two Necks, the Bell and Crown or the Golden Cross via Piccadilly were changed for tougher creatures who could cope with the rough and tumble of the country roads. At night they might well be "a blind 'un, a bolter, and two good kickers".

In the 1820s the first stage was extended to Hounslow resulting in a decline in the Red Cow's coaching side of the business. However, the landlords were enterprising, so the trade just changed and became a favourite pull-up for the waggoners, passing in the early hours of the morning with their produce for Covent Garden, and on their return they would call in for perhaps a tankard of ale and a slice of cheese.

The line of coaches, still six in all but with Quicksilver now in the lead, hurried along the Chiswick High Road towards Turnham Green. Turnham Green possessed not one but two commons – the rear one, called Turnham Bec and the front common, the Green. Around the Green stood some fine 17th and 18th century red brick mansions, each one secluded within its high garden walls. Turnham Green was an attractive spot with orchards, market gardens, open meadows and farms.

Standing alongside the road was the Old Pack Horse. It was here that Sir George Barclay and a man called Perkins, plotted the assassination of King William III in February, 1696. They were the ringleaders and in the pay of the exiled James II and the plan was for a band of forty men under their leadership to surround the king's carriage as he returned from hunting in Richmond Park. The carriage would be making for Kensington Palace, and in a narrow and muddy lane, near where Turnham Green church now stands, the vehicle had to slow to a walking pace. Somehow the king was informed and many of the band were arrested and the leaders executed. This plot could so easily have succeeded and the whole course of our history would have been changed. The Old Pack Horse was demolished about 1900.

From Turnham Green to Brentford past the turning for Kew Bridge. The Romans had established a crossing point of the Thames at Brentford and it had witnessed battles in the time of both Canute and Charles I, but in the 1820s was just a small, peaceful market town. The Mails drove straight down the High Street although other coaches and post-chaise might change at the Pigeons, Catherine Wheel or the Green Dragon. Leaving Brentford they passed close to Syon House, the seat of the Dukes of North-umberland, the early history of which is a succession of tragedies and disasters. Edward Seymour, Duke of Somerset, built the house within the older walls of a nunnery but was executed before its completion. His successors fared little better in the short reign of Lady Jane Grey. During the Civil War the house was for a time a prison for the children of Charles I. Later, Canaletto produced a fine picture of the exterior and Robert Adam turned the interior into one of his masterpieces.

As they reached Strawberry Green, Quicksilver's guard would sound his horn to warn the gatekeeper at the toll house to open wide the gate. As gatekeepers could be in serious trouble if they delayed the Mails, he would have kept the gate open for the other five coaches a little way behind.

A mile further on Hounslow was reached. Then it was a military town and an extensive coaching stage – the first out of town. They stabled over 2,000 horses there, a considerable number of which were kept at the George, the Red Lion and the Golden Cross.

A change of horse was an exercise in precision. Ostlers unhar-nessed the leaders and wheelers which had brought the coach from Piccadilly and led them to their stalls. Other ostlers harnessed the fresh team. The wheelers were the two horses nearest the coach. The leaders, usually lighter, more active horses, led the team. In two or three minutes the coach was off again.

Leaving Hounslow the road divides. Fork right for Bath and Bristol, straight on for Exeter. No coachman now would recognise it, although part of the old toll house still stood at the junction around the turn of the century. The three coaches for Devonport,

Exeter and Poole would head for Staines; the other three for Bath, Bristol and Gloucester would turn for Maidenhead.

Quicksilver, with the fresh team, now began to cross the notorious Hounslow Heath. Most of it lies buried now beneath the runways of London Airport, but then this scrub land, windy and desolate, was associated with names like Claude du Vall, Dick Turpin and Gentleman Harry. Since the onset of the Mails, carrying armed guards, robbing coaches was not quite the business it had been, although it is possible the gibbet still stood on the Heath to serve as a reminder of the price that had to be paid.

After Hounslow Heath the road then followed closely the course of the Roman Way to Silchester, just past the old powder mills at Babe, then through the village of Bedfont with the Black Dog Inn adjacent to the church. By now the sun would have set and darkness fallen.

Through this rather featureless landscape of level ground good coaching horses in an extended trot could for some time keep up a speed of eleven to twelve miles an hour. Even in midsummer it would have been dark unless there was moonlight. To the outsider sitting on the box beside the coachman, a very favoured position, all that would have been visible would be the dim outline of the leaders and the wheelers partly lit by the lamps of the coach. For this reason greys were favoured as part of the team, and if two greys and two darker horses, possibly bays or dark chestnuts, were harnessed, it would be referred to as a "cross-team".

Quite suddenly the vague outline of the hedges alongside the road gave way to houses and, as they drove up the High Street of Staines and with no regard whatsoever to the sleeping inhabitants, the guard sounded his horn to warn the ostlers at the Market House of the approach of the Royal Mail. The Devonport coach was due at four minutes to ten o'clock. The Exeter and Poole coaches were not due until twenty minutes later.

From Staines across the River Thames and towards Egham Town renowned then for its famous race meetings in August and September. George IV often attended to make it a royal occasion.

After Egham the road passes over Englefield Heath, past Virginia Water, an artificial lake of some considerable extent created about the middle of the 18th century by the then Duke of Cumberland. He was at that time Ranger to the Windsor Great Park.

Egham Common, Shrubs Hill, past the well-known Cricketers Inn and then over Bagshot Heath to the town itself. Here a stop at the King's Arms to change the horses, having covered twenty-six miles from Hyde Park Corner, and they would leave the inn at ten minutes past eleven. Up the road which climbs steeply out of the town the new team proceeded at a good pace to a point at the top of the hill where stood the Golden Farmer (today the Jolly Farmer). The left hand road leads to Farnham, Alton and Winchester.

In this inn, towards the end of the 17th century, there lived one William Davies. Well respected in the district he was a man who paid promptly, well and always in gold. One night a coach was robbed on Bagshot Heath, possibly as it lumbered up the hill. There was nothing new in this as many coaches were robbed as they crossed this heath! This particular highwayman always handed back all jewellery and notes, keeping only the coin. Unfortunately on this occasion, after he had returned all but the gold, one of the travellers shot him in the back. Wounded, he was captured, bound hand and foot and hauled back to the doorway of the King's Arms at Bagshot. There the local worthies recognised the "gentleman" as William Davies alias the Golden Farmer. Though he had been held in high esteem the law was the law and he was hanged and afterwards gibbeted on his own threshold.

First through Camberley and Yorktown and a quick change at the White Hart in Blackwater. Climbing out of the one long street of this town, Quicksilver would come to the Hartford Bridge flats. Wild, open country and six miles of "good galloping ground". So at the top of the hill a crack of the whip and they were off in a fast canter. Thundering into the darkness with the dim shapes of the cantering horses lit from the lamp under the footrest, it was quite exciting and also pleasant if on a warm June night. However, to be an outsider in winter with lashing rain and high winds would doubtless make many think otherwise.

The team travelled quickly to Hartford Bridge, and after crossing a brick bridge, built in 1707, over the River Hart they drew up at the White Lion. King George III, in the days when he took his family for holidays at Weymouth, used to stop there for breakfast.

If the guard had checked his timepiece and the coach was up to schedule after passing through Hartney Row and heading for Murrell Green, it would have been three-and-three-quarter hours from the time it left Hyde Park Corner. The distance is thirty-eight miles.

Quicksilver had to cover over 213 miles to Devonport including all stops in twenty-four hours. This had to allow for twenty change of horse and just under an hour for two meals, and by 1836 they had improved the time still further. Yet in 1752 when the stagecoach, the Exeter Fly, was put on the road, it took three days from Exeter to London and the proprietors, to cover themselves, always added to their advertisement "If God be willing". God could then be blamed if in bad weather it took six days!

Still greater progress had been made since the late 17th century, when the huge hooded waggons of Russell & Co. left Falmouth with a team of eight draught horses and finally ambled in to London some twelve to fourteen days later. It was said that a man on a "pony" rode beside the team with a long whip which was used to touch the horses up from time to time and thus try to keep some

23

sort of schedule. In summer the roads were bad enough; in winter almost impassable. It is strange to think that the passengers walked! It was their luggage that was carried in the waggon and at night they slept beneath the waggon or, in winter, the stable lofts of the inns en route.

In the 1820s, Russell & Co. still plied the route starting at Friday Street, Cheapside, but their "Fly Vans" then covered the journey from London to Exeter via Andover, Salisbury and Shaftesbury in two days. Their passengers were no longer content to walk although they did not disdain travelling amongst the bales and bundles which made up the bulk of the cargo because the fare, about 1s. per day, was so very reasonable.

Although there was an article in the *London Weekly Review* of August, 1828 praising Mr. Gurney's steam coach as:

> . . . this beautiful specimen of mechanical invention appears at length to be brought to a state of perfection beyond which we hardly think it possible to make any essential improvement.

it never rivalled the coaches. Steam on the railway did that.

The road to Basingstoke was easy on the horses although the slight climb through Hook past the White Hart would have slowed the pace a little before they trotted down to Mapledurwell Hatch and on towards Basingstoke. Near the outskirts of this town was Chineham House where the celebrated Chief Superintendent of Mails, Thomas Hasker, spent his retirement. From 1792 to 1817 this great organiser had been responsible for the Royal Mail service. Reading his instructions to the guards, and letters of complaint when matters went wrong, one realises how much his example of discipline and devotion to the service inspired all who worked both directly and indirectly for him and resulted in the high standard achieved by the Royal Mails at the time, making the British postal service the envy of the world.

Another change of horse at Basingstoke, possibly at the Crown. *Cary's Great Roads of England and Wales* quotes "Basingstoke is a corporate town of some 601 houses and 3165 inhabitants". From Basingstoke to Andover through Overton and Whitchurch. The village of Deane lies about half a mile to the north of this road. Jane Austen's father was the incumbent there, although they lived at Steventon Rectory. This is where she wrote a number of her novels including *Sense and Sensibility* and *First Impressions*, later re-named *Pride and Prejudice*.

The valley now broadens out into flat meadows with rushes, alders and hazels beside the River Test which eventually flows into Southampton Water. The bridge over the river here is a small yet elegant iron structure. The cottages beside the river are of flint and brick construction with thatched roofs.

Quicksilver trotted smartly towards Whitchurch, which at the time was a small borough town sending two Members of Parliament to Westminster. The 1832 Reform Act altered this anomaly. Whitchurch was the intersection of the London to Exeter and Southampton to Oxford roads, so the White Hart was a coaching establishment of some magnitude. Here also was a silk mill erected in the 18th century which is still operating today.

Although the arrival at the White Hart was just after two o'clock in the early hours of the morning, ostlers had to be ready for the change. There was not a minute to waste, and then the coach pressed on to Andover.

The Devonport Mail called at the Star and Garter for passengers, assuming there were any, at three o'clock in the morning, although the mail for Andover itself was carried by the Exeter coach. This did not arrive until an hour later. At this time all the postal business in the town was transacted at the Star and Garter by Jane Mercer, the postmistress. A directory published in 1823 states that the Mail left Andover, from the White Hart at Bridge Street, for London at ten o'clock each evening and for the West at four o'clock in the morning.

Stage coaches left Andover for London, Exeter, Barnstaple, Taunton, Salisbury, Southampton and Weymouth. It was an important town with a population in the 1820s of over 4,000. Many of these people were employed in the malting trade, the manufacture of shalloons (a light cloth used in linings) and the coach and staging business. Of those concerned with the latter, there were twenty-four innkeepers, two licensed to let post horses, a coach maker, a horse dealer, a turnpike keeper and two common carriers. The long distance carriers, Russell & Co., maintained a large warehouse at Andover and there were at the time many local carriers working to Bath, Bristol, Salisbury, Winchester, Southampton, etc., on various days of the week.

It must have been a great blow to the town when, in 1844, the Mails to Exeter were sent by train. Thirteen years later the London and South Western Railway opened the Andover and Salisbury line, thus driving the last coaches in this district off the road.

After 1836 the Devonport coach travelled over the "top" road via Amesbury and Wincanton. Not far out of Andover on the Amesbury road is Weyhill, where once a year around Old Michaelmas they held a six day fair. The sheep sales are recorded as handling up to 150,000 sheep. One day was the Hop Fair when brewers came from far and wide to buy Farnham and Petersfield hops. Another day was the Mop Fair when the hiring took place for a further year. The farm servants, known as Molls and Johns, offered themselves for hire, and bargained with the farmers. When finally the wage was agreed the men would fix coloured ribbons to their hats and receive an advance of pay. Some spent it all in too much drinking,

so had to walk home when sober. Every day was the Horse Fair –
horses, thousands of them. Many from Ireland, driven all the way
from Holyhead or Milford Haven, taking perhaps over two weeks
on the journey. There were horses from Scotland, Yorkshire and
the Eastern counties. Horses to be harnessed to stage waggon,
farm waggon, post chaise or gig. Although the dealers sold the best
horses as they journeyed down to Weyhill, there were always
plenty to choose from.

Thomas Hardy describes this fair in the opening chapters of *The
Mayor of Casterbridge*.

Quicksilver, however, would have taken the Salisbury road –
over the Wallops. This was an exposed and lonely road and not a
pleasant stage in gales, torrential rain, fog or snow. In periods of
heavy snowfalls it must have been impossible for coaches to travel
between Andover and Salisbury. Even today the road is still vul-
nerable to drifting. For the coach this was the worst enemy of all. In
level snow up to a foot deep they could keep going with six to eight
horses, but drifting meant losing the track of the road and finally
the coach came to a halt. Then the guard must unharness a horse
and ride to the next stage for assistance, carrying the mails if
possible. On the road travelling westward the next staging point
was the Winterslow Hut (now the Pheasant Inn). A lonely spot but
it seems to have appealed to Hazlitt, for he spent some years there.
Perhaps he enjoyed the isolation of the place. Pollard's picture of
the lioness and the Exeter Coach outside the inn is quite well
known and the building was for many years much the same as he
portrayed it, with the horse pond beside the road under a clump of
trees and the stables at the rear. These were quite extensive and
constructed of wooden weather board and thatch.

The road to Salisbury then climbs over Thorney Down, and as
they descended on a summer morning outsiders on the coach
would get their first view of the city nestling in the valley with the
tall spire of this fine cathedral pointing like a finger to the sky.

Over St. Thomas' bridge and on into the city itself. A quick
change at the Black Horse, and the Devonport coach having
already covered eighty miles turned westwards. It crossed the
bridge over the River Avon through Fisherton and down the road
towards Wilton. A level four miles until it reached this town which
was once the capital of Saxon Wessex. Today it is associated with
carpets and its famous house, the home of the Earls of Pembroke.
The house had its origins in the once great Abbey of Wilton, which
was given to the first Earl of Pembroke in 1544, and he built his
home in Tudor style but very little of this remains today. Inigo

OPPOSITE PAGE
*Leaving the Star
and Garter,
Andover*

Jones, with the assistance of his nephew, John Webb, transformed
it into one of his great masterpieces. The rooms, including the
single and double cube rooms are magnificent, but Wilton possesses a unique charm in the view of the house from the Palladian

bridge over the River Nadder, which was not constructed until 1737.

After Wilton the road passes through the village of Barford St. Martins and on to Fovant. Here the Lord Pembroke Arms maintained a fair stable in these times, being half-way between Salisbury and Shaftesbury. To the south of this road is a long line of hills with names such as White Sheet Hill, Fovant Down and Compton Down. Before the lower road was turnpiked in the mid-18th century, along this exposed ridge ran the main road to Salisbury.

On the present road there are still a few of the old milestones, and the one near Donhead reads:

Sarum XV   Shaston V

At Donhead the inn, called once the Arundel Arms, doubtless with respect to Lord Arundel who then lived at Wardour Castle, is at the bottom of a short steep hill. Here they stabled horses for staging. Between here and Ludwell is another steep climb and descent, and the Black Dog there was also a posting inn. From Ludwell to the turnpike gate on the outskirts of Shaftesbury is three miles.

The town stands on a spur commanding wonderful views of the Blackmoor Vale. Here was no castle but an abbey founded in the late part of the 9th century. Because it was the shrine of Edward the Martyr, murdered at Corfe by his stepmother, Elfrida, pilgrims flocked to it. Canute died there, although he was buried at Winchester. Royal patronage made it a wealthy abbey, and the abbess ranked as a baroness. Not even the fact that the abbey had given hospitality to Katherine of Aragon could save it from its fate at the Dissolution, and now only the foundations remain.

Quicksilver arrived at thirty-five minutes past six in the morning at the Grosvenor, which is a fine Georgian building. Twenty minutes was allowed for breakfast, and the coachman who took over at Andover would have announced "Gentlemen, I leave you now" and then waited for the passengers to offer the customary tip. Half a crown for insiders, and 2s. for those on the outside. Usually on journeys not exceeding fifteen hours the guard would remain with the coach throughout, but as Quicksilver's journey took twenty-four hours a change was necessary, and this very probably took place at Shaftesbury. It was the guard's duty to see that the timesheet was properly completed and he would have handed this over to his successor who, in his turn, continued to record the times of arrival at the various stages before handing it over to the postmaster at Plymouth.

Of course the guard also expected to be tipped, so with this business and the cost of breakfast, passengers left Shaftesbury at least 7s. the poorer.

2 The Devonport Mail (Quicksilver)

The journey from Shaftesbury to Devonport

Even at this early hour, between half past six and seven o'clock in the morning, inns like the Grosvenor were busy, noisy, places. Apart from providing breakfast for the passengers on the Mail, there would be other travellers who had slept the night, anxious to start as early as possible on the next stage of their respective journeys. Post-chaise to be horsed, a fresh team for the Mail, kept ostlers busy. The hoofs of excited horses clattered on the cobbles.

Robert Southey described this scene in *Letters from England* and although the actual inn concerned is near Falmouth, apart from mention of the packets, it is applicable to any hostelry in the country:

> The perpetual stir and bustle in this inn is as surprising as it is wearisome. Doors opening and shutting, bells ringing, voices calling to the waiter from every quarter, while he cries "coming," to one room, and hurries away to another. Everybody is in a hurry here; either they are going off in packets, and are hastening their preparations to embark; or they have just arrived, and are impatient to be on the road homeward. Every now-and-then a carriage rattles up to the door with a rapidity which makes the very house shake. The man who cleans the boots is running in one direction, the barber with his powder-bag in another; here goes the barber's boy with his hot water and razors; there comes the clean linen from the washer-woman; and the hall is full of porters and sailors bringing in luggage, or bearing it away; now you hear a horn blow because the post is coming in, and in the middle of the night you are awakened by another because it is going out. Nothing is done in England without a noise, and yet noise is the only thing they forget in the bill!

The arrival and departure of the Mail, at least during daylight hours, was always an event in the daily life of the town's inhabitants resulting in a cluster of spectators who were able to spare the time to watch Quicksilver leave on its journey to the west.

The first task of the new team was to take the coach down the very steep hill at Enmore Green. The skid was placed under the nearside rear wheel of the coach which prevented it from turning. The wheelers also had to be strong enough to hold the coach from gathering too much momentum during the descent. At the bottom

*A Britzechka
passes the
Mermaid, Yeovil*

the coach stopped. The guard removed the skid and they proceeded to cross the Blackmoor Vale, flat open country referred to by Thomas Hardy as "the valley of the little dairies". It still is.

Across the River Stour, flowing between East and West Stour, and the Mail proceeded to Henstridge Ash. A change of horse at the Virginia Inn standing on the crossroads. Here it is said Sir Walter Raleigh's servant emptied a flagon of ale over his master, who was smoking, in the belief that he was on fire!

The road continues westward through Milborne Port, a village now but once a port or borough sending two members to Westminster.

Just before entering Sherborne one can still see the ruins of its castle – and memories of Sir Walter Raleigh. The coach did not pass through the centre of the town, clustered around the abbey church, but kept on the top road to change at the Angel, Green Hill. So outsiders had to be content with a distant glimpse of the tower of Sherborne Abbey church. It was founded in 998. Roger Caen, Henry I's chief minister, and Bishop of Salisbury, pulled down the Saxon cathedral to replace it with a much larger Norman abbey. In the mid-15th century, the new choir was built in Perpendicular style and later the nave with the outstanding fan-vaulted roof, considered one of the finest in the country, was added. At the Dissolution the abbey was given to Sir John Horsey, who sold it to the town. The abbey became the parish church, and many of the monastery buildings were leased to Sherborne School and later incorporated into it. They still remain, altered over the years, in harmony with the 13th century almshouses.

The road between Sherborne and Yeovil was then by way of Nether Compton and crossed the River Yeo near the town itself. There were three fine old inns here, the Three Choughs, the George, and the Mermaid where the Royal Mails called. Three miles west of Yeovil the coach passed the London Inn at Pye Corner and drove on to East Chinnock. The coachman needed to know this ground well for on the short hills there was ample opportunity to "spring the team". This was an art that needed both courage and experience. The coach was allowed to descend without the use of the skid and just before it reached the bottom of the hill, the horses were encouraged to canter; the coach rushed down a short way and this gave the team sufficient impetus to pull it up the next hill for quite a distance before they slowed back into a trot.

At half past ten in the morning they were due at the George at Crewkerne, which externally is relatively unchanged since the Mails called here.

According to a report in the *Taunton Courier* in February, 1828, "letters have on numerous occasions remained in the Post Office at Crewkerne and could not be forwarded to Ilminster until the following day. . . .".

31

The report went on, "On a recent occasion a letter was forwarded from Plymouth intimating that the Duke of Clarence would be at the George at Ilminster at an appointed time".

Unfortunately the duke and his suite arrived at the hotel to find no arrangements had been made for them as the letter concerned was still at the post office in Crewkerne. Obviously the heir to the throne was far from pleased for almost immediately afterwards a change was made by the Post Office to ensure Ilminster received its mail the same day that it was delivered to Crewkerne.

The steep hill out of the town on the road to the west would have required two additional horses. These would be unharnessed at the top to return to the town while the coach travelled along the 700 feet high ridge towards Chard. From this road there are extensive views of the Somerset vale to the north and parts of Devon and Dorset to the south.

They reached Chard at a quarter to twelve after the long descent from Windwistle to change again at the George in Fore Street. In the 16th and 17th centuries Chard was an assize town on the western circuit. Records show that the judges who rode the circuit, accompanied by their clerks and servants, resided during their visit to the town not at the local inn but at the houses of the local gentry. It would appear that the standard of entertainment they required was of a high order and many sent presents to the host of game, fish, fowl and even cheeses and wine to assist him in the task of providing suitable hospitality for their Lordships.

The Mail, after leaving Chard, took the road through Stockland to Monkton, which is not the way most people travel today between Chard and Honiton. It had the great advantage that it was straight.

At the Golden Lion in Honiton, as arrival was scheduled for five minutes to one, it was time for dinner. Twenty-five minutes was allowed, but there was always the chance that if they were late the guard might try to curtail this a little. Here he had a problem because he was held responsible for good timekeeping, yet if he upset the passengers, he might find them less generous with tips. At this time the long wide street of the town contained over fifty inns, including the Angel and the Dolphin. Although with so many routes converging on Honiton the coaching business then was the mainstay of the town, it had not always been so. In the 17th and early 18th centuries Honiton was renowned for its lace, but unfortunately by the beginning of the last century this industry began to decline due to the introduction of machinery. This led to a petition for "Royal favour to aid the distressed lace workers of the district" being made to Queen Adelaide. She, and later Queen Victoria, gave limited patronage to this industry and one of Queen Victoria's lace gowns is said to have cost £1,000.

The Exeter road follows for a while the course of the River Otter.

This is very attractive country with small farms, thatched cottages and orchards, small grazing paddocks surrounded by deciduous trees, and fields which when ploughed reveal deep red soil. In dry weather on these unmetalled roads, dust was always a problem to those on top of the coach. For most of the journey it would have been chalky white but now it was red in colour as it swirled around the coach which moved swiftly on this easy road to Fairmile. At this inn they made the last change before reaching Exeter. Any time lost would have to be made up now as they pushed on past Rockbeare through the village of Honiton Clyst, with its church tower built in red sandstone, down the long street of Heavitree. The Mail was due at the New London Inn, Exeter, at ten minutes to three in the afternoon. This extensive hostelry, built in 1794, was the largest in the west of England, with stabling for up to 300 horses. It stood not far from the crossing between High Street and Sidwell Street and was not demolished until the 1930s, to make way for a cinema. The luxury of the interior impressed Robert Southey on a visit in 1802, and throughout the last century it was the centre of political and social life in the city.

The Mail coach would have brought copies of the previous day editions of the London papers for use in the two reading rooms of this establishment. Most papers of the time cost between 6d. and 7d., a penny less for innkeepers.

Fresh horses, a change of coachman, a possible change in some of the passengers, and they would have set off again. Ahead of them lay forty-five miles of quite hilly country. They trotted down the High Street, across the new Exe Bridge built in 1778, and then on through the village of Alphington. Before 1823 the road to Chudleigh was a rough track through Shillingford and over Bullers Hill. The new road went over Haldon Moor. Somewhere at the bottom of this hill, possibly at Woodlands where later a toll house was erected, they must have kept additional horses to assist in pulling vehicles up this steep gradient. At the top of Haldon is a magnificent view of not only the city of Exeter but also the whole of the Exe estuary. Having overcome the problem of getting up the hill, they had to slowly descend again. After this the road was an easy one into Chudleigh. In the long main street is the Clifford Arms (now the Old Coaching House) which externally has changed little since the early days of the last century. The Duke and Duchess of Clarence stayed there on more than one occasion, and amongst other notable guests was the Princess Royal of France, daughter of Louis XVI, who resided at the inn for some time after fleeing from France.

Another change of horse. The coach had now travelled 175 miles since leaving London. Although there had been great improvements to the surface of the roads in the 1820s, they were still rough in places. The pace was fast and the wear and tear on the vehicle considerable, yet breakdowns, which had to be recorded, were not too frequent. The main reason was the excellent design and construction of the mail coach and the regular maintenance by Vidlers of Millbank. As they were all of the same design, parts were interchangeable. Official instructions to guards issued by the Post Office in 1815 made certain that they were able to carry out minor repairs. "Guards must have a wrench, cord chain, wheel clips, shackle perch bolt, drift pin, nails, screwdriver, worms and screws, and also a double or long spreading bar". A complete do-it-yourself kit. On the lonely stretches of road which the Mails travelled, they could well be useful.

On their way to Ashburton they passed through Knighton over Jews Bridge and Beckington, to stop for another change at the Golden Lion. They could waste no time so after about two minutes the wheels began to turn again. First through Buckfastleigh, where the old abbey was still in ruins, and then the coach took the upper road to Harbourneford. Some would get a glimpse of Dean Prior church, whose vicar in the 17th century was the poet Robert Herrick. Just a minute or so before six o'clock they reached Ivybridge to draw up at the hotel. W. G. Maton wrote of the town and this establishment at the turn of the 18th century:

> Ivy-bridge is a small group of houses delightfully situated on the banks of the river Arme, which rushes with a loud roar over a bed of rocks; after a rainy season it forms quite a torrent, and brings down from the hills fragments of granite. The rocks which constitute its bed seem to have been torn and hurled, as it were, from their original situations by some paroxysm of nature. Close to the bridge stands one of the most comfortable and elegant inns in the west of England, and in the gardens belonging to it (which run along one side of the river) the bridge, the high grounds beyond it, the rocks, and the foaming current assume the most picturesque relations.

Outside the hotel the old narrow hump-backed bridge still remains, so it is not difficult to imagine the skill required to negotiate it driving a coach and four horses.

The next stop would have been the George at Ridgway Plympton.

Although unofficial stops at inns were discouraged, they obviously took place if the guard agreed. On one occasion the Bath/Devonport Mail was left unattended outside an inn some seven miles from the King's Arms at Plymouth. The horses grew tired of waiting while the coachman and guard enjoyed their drinks, so they set off on their own. The only outsider was a Mrs. Cox, a fishwife from Devonport, who tried unsuccessfully to attract the attention of some passers-by. She was wise enough not to scream

Fore Street,
Devonport

in case she frightened the horses. On they trotted, negotiating all hazards including a bridge and all oncoming traffic. Even the tollgate keeper at Crabtree had the gate open for them. One wonders just what he thought as the coach passed through without a coachman or guard! Dead on time, they came to a halt outside the King's Arms, and the insiders were amazed when they alighted to find that the horses had accomplished this stage on their own.

Quicksilver followed the same route to Plymouth through Marsh Mills, where there was frequent flooding, to Lipson and then passed the King's Arms in Briton Side to the Post Office in Bilbury Street. Here was delivered the Plymouth mail.

It took a quarter of an hour to trot down Union Street over Stonehouse Bridge and up to Fore Street, Devonport, to Elliott's Royal Hotel and the end of the journey. They had completed a journey of 213 miles in just twenty-four hours.

Any passengers travelling to Cornwall would stay the night at the Elliott's Royal Hotel or Weakley's on the opposite side of the street. Then on the following morning at seven o'clock they would be taken by post-chaise, together with the mails, to New Passage to cross the River Tamar by rowing boat to Cornwall. At Torpoint the Royal Cornwall Mail would be waiting to make the journey to Falmouth.

In 1835, however, a steam flat-bottomed barge fifty-five feet long and fifty feet wide was introduced. It could carry four large vehicles at a time as well as the horses. Because of the extensive packet service from Falmouth at this time, the Post Office introduced new schedules so that after a short stop at Devonport the coach drove on to the ferry, crossed and went straight down to Falmouth.

Extract from *Cary's* 1828:

PACKET BOATS

AT FALMOUTH, FOR AMERICA

Mails are made up in London on the first Wednesday in each Month for British North America, Bermuda, and the United States, with which a Packet sails from Falmouth on the Saturday following.

AT FALMOUTH, FOR LISBON

The Mail for Lisbon is made up in London every Tuesday night, and despatched from Falmouth on the Friday following.

AT FALMOUTH FOR MADEIRA AND BRAZIL

The Mail is made up in London the First Tuesday in every Month, and despatched from Falmouth on the Friday following.

3　The Exeter Mail

Travelling by way of Salisbury and Dorchester (starting at Salisbury)

Unlike Quicksilver the Exeter coach had dropped off mail bags at various points all the way to Salisbury, so that the Devonport coach passed through the city almost one and a half hours before the latter arrived.

Today we talk of New Towns but in 1220 such ideas did not exist. Yet Salisbury is new, for the old city with its ancient Celtic earthworks and Norman cathedral, known as Old Sarum, lies two miles to the north now deserted and desolate.

Frequent quarrels between the army garrison and the church, together with the lack of a good supply of water, caused Bishop Poore in 1219 to obtain permission to establish a new city and cathedral. The place chosen was the confluence of the rivers Avon, Nadder and Bourne, and building started in the following year.

Today visitors can still walk in the meadows beside these rivers and pause near the point from which Constable painted the last of his three pictures of this cathedral entitled *Salisbury Cathedral from the Meadows*. One can also recall that Izaak Walton, whose son was a resident canon of the cathedral, must on occasions have spent many pleasant hours here.

Around the year 1265 the main part of the cathedral was completed. The building was constructed in one style of architecture – early English Gothic. The spire, which rises to 404 feet, the tallest in the country, was really an afterthought, as the original designs allowed only for a small central tower. Built between 1334 and 1365 this beautiful addition seems to crown the glory of the whole building.

Bishop Poore's plan for the city was for the streets to be laid out in a simple grid pattern, resulting in dignified order instead of untidy development. A charter for a market was granted in its early days, and much of the prosperity of the city was based on the cloth and wool trade which is reflected in the many fine buildings. The importance of this aspect of its trade must have declined by the middle of the last century, for Anthony Trollope gives a different picture of the city in his Barchester novels.

At the corner of St. John's Street stands the White Hart. This was the most suitable of all the city's many inns and posting houses for those coaches bound for Exeter. The Mail arrived from London just before six o'clock in the morning. Quicksilver had left the city at four thirty-five for Shaftesbury.

The Mail left by way of Exeter Street passing the cathedral and Bishop's Palace to cross the River Avon over Harnham bridge built in 1244.

37

A Cabriolet waits outside the White Hart, Salisbury

Between here and Woodyates was very exposed downland, just gorse, bracken and rabbits, with long views particularly to the east. From the top of the coach all one would see ahead would be the road rising and falling gently. There were very few buildings anywhere so that the arrival at Woodyates would have come as a complete surprise. Here, alongside the road on the right hand side, were extensive high walls of flint on a brick base capped with red tiles with a central entrance by way of a timber archway which opened on to a large quadrangle. This was surrounded by a considerable number of stalls for horses, odd waggon sheds and barns. The inn itself had no name and was just known as Woodyates. It had three high pitched gables, stood back from the road and on the west side of the square of outbuildings. King George III always called here with his family for a meal during his annual visits to Weymouth, and during his stay a special Mail coach was scheduled to serve his needs. It ran between the General Post Office in London to Windsor and on to Weymouth, carrying everything from the State papers to fresh vegetables. It called at Woodyates at three o'clock in the morning.

For three generations the same family, the Brownings, owned Woodyates and were the forefathers of the poet Robert Browning. Today only one short length of wall remains at Woodyates. Next a long climb to the top of Handley Hill. Here the view is quite magnificent in every direction. To the north are glimpses of the vast Cranbourne Chase, renowned still for its beech and oak, although never quite the same after the extensive felling during the wars with Napoleon. This great estate of more than 750,000 acres was given by James I to William Cecil.

The signpost here read "6d. Handley 1 mile". The name of the village is actually Sixpenny Handley. The road descends gently to Tarrant Hinton through undulating country past signposts with names like Wimborne St. Giles, Gussage St. Michael, Long Crichel and Chettle. Down to Pimperne and in just over two miles is Blandford.

Blandford, like Marlborough, as the result of many serious fires, has a splendid wide main street. On 4th June, 1731, occurred the most serious of them all, destroying most of the town, and the following is an account from the town records:

This Dreadful Fire broke out about 2 in the afternoon in a Thatched house (in Salisbury Street) being a Tallow Chandlers, at which time the Wind blew strong at N. West which carried the Flame ever towards the East end of the Church, and set fire to all the buildings in that Tract, so that not less than 20 houses were on fire within a $\frac{1}{4}$ of an hour. The Wind soon shifted from N. West to North, which hurried the Flames aloft that once fired the other Parts of the Town with ye adjacent Villages of Briantstone and

Blandford St. Mary, so that all before the Wind in the space of an hour was on Fire, and the Thatched buildings soon consumed. The stronger parts of the Town remained till towards Night, but all the intermediate space between the Houses, Streets etc. were so hot that above 16 Persons lost their Lives in the Flames. The Church by the care of some of the Inhabitants was preserved till about 11 at night, tho' the Spire which was covered with Lead took fire within side about 4 in the afternoon which was soon extinguished, but the fire flying over and thro' it at every Crevice, some sparks where-of lay latent till abt 2 in the morning then broke out in the middle Isle under the lead, where twas impossible to extinguish it without Engines which were already burnt many hours before and the Inhabitants so tired with fatigues that before morning ye Church really destroyed ye poor remains being scarcely fit for a Foundation.

Two brothers, John and William Bastard, were responsible for the rebuilding of this town, which was completed in the space of about thirty years. Consequently it provides an outstanding example of an 18th century market town.

Under an Act of Parliament, a Court of Record was set up to lay down rules for the rebuilding of the town. Apart from a new church completed in 1739, there was a town hall, two new inns, and the plan allowed for three different types of houses for different classes of townspeople, the wealthy merchants and professional men, the shopkeepers and the artisans.

In 1760 when most of this rebuilding had been completed, they erected a Fire Monument which stands against the churchyard wall and part of the inscription acknowledges "Divine Mercy which has raised this town from its ashes". The principal inns were the Red Lion, Greyhound and the Crown which was rebuilt in the 1930s.

The Mails changed at the Crown. In 1796 Mr. Hasker, Chief Superintendent of Mails, must have realised the reliability of the landlords for he entrusted to them the responsibility of holding a spare Mail coach in case of need during the period of the king's stay at Weymouth.

After changing horses the coach proceeded across the splendid stone bridge over the River Stour and trotted smartly up the first hill on its way to Dorchester. There is no record they changed horses until they reached Dorchester, a distance of sixteen miles, but as the Cardinal's Cap at Milborne kept post-horses it is possible a change was made here. It is a road of ups and downs and at the crossroads for Dewlish there existed at this time a turnpike gate. At the King's Arms at Puddletown – then known as Piddletown and the Weatherbury of Hardy's novel *Far from the Madding Crowd* – the royal Weymouth coach made its last change, but the Exeter Mail did not pause in this attractive little village.

40

Then on to Troy Town, over Yellowdown Hill across Grey's Bridge to enter Dorchester itself. They drove up the High East Street past the White Hart and houses and shops described so well in Hardy's story *The Mayor of Casterbridge*:

> The agricultural and pastoral character of the people upon whom the town depended for its existence was shown by the class of objects displayed in the shop windows. Scythes, reap-hooks, sheep-shears, bill-hooks, spades, mattocks, and hoes at the ironmonger's; beehives, butter-firkins, churns, milking stools and pails, hay-rakes, field-flagons, and seed-lips at the cooper's; cart-ropes and plough-harness at the saddler's; carts, wheelbarrows, and mill-gear at the wheelwright's and machinist's; horse-embrocations at the chemist's; at the glover's and leather-cutter's, hedging-gloves, thatcher's knee-caps, ploughman's leggings, villager's pattens and clogs.

Just short of the Cross stands the King's Arms, a noble building with graceful circular bay windows, pillared entrance and, at the rear at that time, extensive stabling.

Dorchester is an ancient garrison town – the Durnovaria of the Romans. Even then they realised the strategic importance of the position of this town in the event of any invasion of the district. During the Napoleonic wars this was still appreciated and Dorchester was once again very much a garrison town. In the year before Trafalgar the garrison and all the defences were alerted one summer morning because through the sea mist surrounding Portland ships were sighted creeping slowly towards the coast. The royal family were at Weymouth. It was a case of action stations. Men from the Dorchester garrisons were despatched with urgency to man the defences in Portland, Weymouth and the beach at Chesil. The royal family had to be evacuated at once so they sent to Blandford for the spare coach. There was much activity as the morning sun gradually cleared the mists away to reveal the Weymouth fishing boats quietly coming home with their haul!

This incident may well be forgotten now but Dorchester still remembers how Judge Jeffries held a special Assize Court in September, 1685 in the town. Just the suspicion, just the fact that you could not prove that you were at home during the battle at Sedgmoor was sufficient to condemn you to death, or transportation for life. Jeffries executed some seventy-four simple country folk who had been persuaded to join the Cause, and transported the better part of two hundred at this court alone. The heads of those executed were impaled on the railings of St. Peter's Church as a fearful warning against insurrection.

Just after leaving the King's Arms one passes St. Peter's Church. In the porch of this church is a memorial to the Reverend John

White, Rector of the Parish from 1605 until 1648. He led the Dorset emigrants who sailed on the *Mary and John* in 1630 to America where they founded the colony which eventually became Massachusetts.

Continuing up the High West Street one notices on a wall the words "Hyde Park Corner 120. Blandford 16. Bridport 15".

For about a mile out of Dorchester the road to the west was lined with elm trees planted by prisoners during the Napoleonic wars. At the end of this avenue of trees there is a fine view of Maiden Castle, reputed to be one of the largest earthwork fortifications in Europe, the perimeter of which is over two miles in extent. It was old when the Romans came.

Down to Winterbourne Abbas, through a pleasant valley known locally as Winterbourne Bottom, before starting the steep climb to the crossroads leading to Long Bredy on the left and Maiden Newton on the right. Here there used to stand the Long Bredy gate and the Hut Inn, where a fresh team took over. First to the top of Askerswell Down, and here is a fine view of the English Channel and looking back the outline of the Isle of Portland and the curve of the Chesil Beach. To the north lies Eggerton Hill, another old fortified camp, and all around undulating downs where farmers still maintain large flocks of sheep.

The coachman steadied the team at this point, as ahead lay the long descent past the Travellers' Rest Inn to Bridport. Somewhere on this stretch of road the up and down Exeter Mails would have passed. The guards sounded their horns and the coachmen saluted each other with their whips. Possibly some passengers smiled and waved and others just stared.

Apart from the city of Exeter, Bridport was the largest town on the route from Salisbury, for according to *Cary* in 1828, at "the last census" it possessed 604 houses and 3,742 inhabitants. That was more than Basingstoke. The reason could well be its many industries, boat building, the making of sailcloth, ropes, nets and twine and also fishing, and to a certain extent coaching.

Bridport possesses a very wide street, in which still stands the Bull. Here the coaches would have stopped for thirty minutes for dinner. The inn was purchased in 1701 and owned by a charitable trust set up by a Quaker, one Daniel Taylor. The rent was used to administer the school and to pay the schoolmaster. Also it was in this town in 1651, amongst great excitement, that Charles II was so nearly captured while trying to escape to France disguised as a groom. An ostler at the Old George Inn recognised the king in a town full of Parliamentary troops and only Charles's quick thinking saved his life. He and his party had to leave in a hurry.

In the hall of many of the inns where the Mail coaches called a plain looking clock hung on the wall. Upon the arrival of the coach the guard would be asked for the time as shown by his timepiece,

OPPOSITE PAGE
Arriving at the
King's Arms,
Dorchester

which had been set at the General Post Office in London the evening before. This would ensure that at least one clock in the town was correct though at this time, apart from the coachmen, no one was particularly concerned about the right time. Sunset and sunrise were all that mattered, but from this point onwards gradually time became a more compelling factor in our everyday lives.

After passing through Chideock, they drove by way of Markham Lane to Charmouth. Because of the steepness of the hills between here and Axminster two extra horses would be attached at the George. Half-way up the hill the Lyme Regis road bears to the left but the Axminster road still climbs until the hamlet at Penn is reached.

Here one leaves Dorset for Devon to arrive at Axminster, which *Cary's* describes as "a clean neat Town and has a considerable Manufactory for carpets". It was also occupied by the Duke of Monmouth a day or so after he had landed at Lyme Regis.

During the Napoleonic War cards were issued to all the inhabitants of Axminster, of which the following is a copy:

> Axminster District Card No..........
> Place of Meeting....................

In case of Enemy Landing in this neighbourhood or orders being received for the removal of the inhabitants, places will be allowed for your family in Mr .... waggon, No .... On your arrival at the place of meeting you are to deliver this card to Mr .... Conductor.
You will be allowed to take with you only .... days provisions and one blanket (marked) for each person. Should places allowed for your family not be sufficient, those that can walk may attach themselves to the same Waggon or Cart, and take their turns to be assisted and must bring provisions and blanket as above.

> R. Hallett Agent
> for Axminster Parish

Bull. Printer.

The coach arrived at the George at a quarter to three – 147 miles from Hyde Park Corner – in eighteen and a quarter hours. Had you travelled all the way you might well have been stiff, but perhaps the views on this delightful coast road would have made it all worthwhile.

Fresh horses and ten miles of ups and downs through Kilmington and Wilmington, and in just over the hour the coach started to descend the long hill past the toll gate to the town of Honiton itself.

After changing horses here the Mail followed the same route as Quicksilver to the city of Exeter. It arrived at the New London Inn just before six o'clock in the evening. The Bath/Exeter Mail was due eighteen minutes later and the Devonport Mail was well on its way to Plymouth. Besides the Mails, stagecoaches, stage waggons, post-chaise and private carriages passed through Exeter day and night.

Its importance was realised in Roman times. Since then both Saxons and Danes in their turn occupied this city beside the River Exe. William the Conqueror personally attacked the place in 1068 and apparently was not too angry with the inhabitants' attempts at resistance, for after the surrender he did not deal too severely with them. He did in fact stay on to rebuild their defences leaving them much stronger than before, as Exeter could be the rear door should the Danes or any other invader attack England from the south-west.

Then for 400 years the bishops, clergy and citizens enjoyed peace. The city grew in size within its red stone walls. The cathedral, first built in Norman times, was gradually converted in the course of a little over a century to a Gothic style, leaving only the twin towers in their original condition. The building is renowned for the overall symmetry of its design, and the beauty of the Gothic vaulting, unbroken through the entire length of both nave and choir.

In September, 1497, Perkin Warbeck appeared at the gates of Exeter demanding his rights, but the citizens did not concede his idea of his claim to the throne. So he attacked the north and east gates of the city, as it was pointless assailing the west because it was guarded by the river and virtually impregnable. The east gate was eventually entered by Perkin's Cornishmen, who after a hard fight were repulsed. The next day his forces tried the north gate, but guns had been added to the city's defences and so they were forced to retreat towards Cullompton in disarray. Perkin Warbeck fled to Beaulieu Abbey. Henry VII was at Woodstock and upon learning the news travelled westwards by way of Bath and Taunton. Finally, Henry entered Exeter in triumph with Warbeck as his prisoner and remained there for the better part of a month. No doubt he praised the citizens for their loyalty and lived at their expense.

Before he left, however, he gave to the city fathers a fine sword which is kept in the Guildhall to this very day.

Half a century later found Exeter a divided city. The strong Puritan element was for Parliament while the Dean and Chapter, backed by many leading merchants, were for the King. In 1643 the mayor, sheriff and five aldermen, all for Parliament, organised the defence of the city during an eleven week siege by Sir John Berkeley. In the end they surrendered to the Royalists.

A year later Charles I sent his Queen Henrietta Maria to Exeter to await the birth of their child. She lived in the town house of the Earl of Bedford. Not long after the birth of the new princess, news arrived that the Earl of Essex was advancing westwards, which caused the Queen to leave for Falmouth and sail for France. The citizens of Exeter were generous and paid for her escape. She left the baby princess with friends in the city and the king (then at Oxford) rode to Exeter to see his new daughter. She was baptised in the cathedral, and after a short stay urging the citizens to give generously towards the cost of his war, he left. Soon the city was besieged by the Parliamentarian General Fairfax, who waited outside its walls for five months. In the end terms for an honourable surrender were agreed and doubtless all the inhabitants were glad of peace.

Wisely Exeter did not become involved in the Monmouth venture and only gave a cool reception to William of Orange as he passed through their city. They realised that trade was more profitable than politics.

About 1793, according to Thomas Hasker's papers, the Exeter guard had the following orders:

> "Leave the water bottle every Friday, Saturday and Monday at Staines, and every Tuesday, Wednesday and Thursday bring it to London, if not ordered to the contrary. . . ."

This referred to a bottle of sea water sent daily from Weymouth via Dorchester for Her Majesty Queen Charlotte.

In the early 1820s, Russell & Co., the carriers, had extensive premises in South Street. They ran waggons daily to and from London and also conveyed goods to all parts of the west of England. Their advertisements guaranteed delivery to all parts of the west country four days after loading in London.

A night in Exeter and at six o'clock in the morning the Mail left again for London.

4 The Bath/Exeter Mail

Travelling by way of Maidenhead, Marlborough, Devizes, Bath, then through Wells, Bridgwater and Taunton

After the parting of the ways at Hounslow, the Mails for Bath, Bristol and Gloucester would have kept fairly well together until they reached Maidenhead. First across the north side of Hounslow Heath, where fog was by then a greater hazard than the highwayman.

Once a traveller on horseback was lost on Hounslow Heath for a time, and wrote afterwards:

> To my delight I saw a man hanging from a gibbet – my pleasure at this prospect was inexpressible for it convinced me I was approaching a civilised community.

Until the early part of the 19th century, highwaymen had been a serious problem when crossing the heath. They seemed to command a certain amount of admiration, at least from those who had not been robbed. A story is told concerning a certain noble lord who had occasion to regularly travel the Bath road, and having been held up a number of times took to arming both his coachman and himself. He did not have to wait long for an attack to be made on his carriage, and when the face appeared at the window with the usual demand fired so quickly that he killed the robber outright. It took some years for society to forgive his lordship this action, for though it was content to see the man hang, they considered shooting him a very unsportsmanlike gesture!

After crossing Cranford Bridge they headed for Colnbrook.

Due in no small measure to the influence of the society who travelled to Bath, the whole length of this road was brought under the turnpike system as early as 1743. It became known as the "Road of Fashion", and Robert Nash arranged that a pump was placed every two miles along the road to provide water to lay the dust in dry seasons. One still exists today at Poyle.

At Colnbrook stands the famous Ostrich Inn. The original building was over 100 years old when King John is reputed to have paused for refreshment there on his way to Runnymede to sign the Magna Carta. Later, in medieval times, a certain landlord and his wife murdered many rich guests. A trap door was placed under the four poster bed in the principal bedroom, which in the middle of the night they operated, ejecting the unsuspecting sleeper into a vat of boiling liquid in the cellar beneath. They took the victim's riches and sold his horse. In the end it was the sale of the horse to someone who became suspicious that led to the discovery of their enterprise.

47

Opposite this inn is a mile post which says:

> London   17
> Hounslow   7
> Maidenhead   9

From Colnbrook to Slough, a quick change of horse, and on towards Maidenhead.

Standing just to the north of the bridge on the outskirts of this town is the Skindles Inn. At one time the landlord there was a fervent Radical and would boast he could command a dozen votes at any election. He also had a good for nothing son who from time to time was an embarrassment. During a certain Berkshire election, a Tory solicitor was staying at the inn and had occasion to go to London on business. On his return his gig was stopped on Hounslow Heath by a highwayman.

"I have no money," stated the lawyer, "but I will give you my gold watch and chain."

"You have a thousand pounds in gold under your seat," came the unexpected reply. "Throw back the apron."

The lawyer obeyed but as the highwayman stooped to take the box quickly knocked the pistol out of his hand and drove off at a gallop. The lawyer had an excellent horse and before the highwayman could find his pistol, which apparently had landed in a ditch, the gig was beyond pursuit.

The next morning the lawyer spoke with the landlord telling him how he was stopped on Hounslow Heath. The landlord was told that the lawyer recognised the highwayman's voice and suggested he might well speak with his son upon the matter. Although the landlord was quite innocent of the whole affair, after confronting his son, he returned to the lawyer to confirm the attack had indeed been made. He then started to plead for him, to be told by the lawyer that he intended to take no further action on one condition.

"You know, Landlord, you have boasted you can command a dozen votes."

"Aye, Sir," came the reply.

"Well then, all you have to do is to arrange that they are given to my side and not yours"! And this indeed was carried out.

The bridge over the River Thames is a splendid structure with fine balustrades and pavements on either side, from which there are excellent views of the river in each direction. To the north at Cookham, in the third week in July, the swans are marked by the King's Swanmaster in a ceremony known as Swan-upping. There are three owners, the Queen, the Dyers Company and the Vintners Company. The last of these three mark their birds with two nicks on the beak, which is believed to be the origin of the name of the inn in Lad Lane, the Swan with Two Necks, which should be the

Swan with Two Nicks, in other words the property of the Vintners Company.

The change at the Sun in Maidenhead took little time and in a few minutes the Gloucester Mail was turning off the Reading road to head for Henley-on-Thames and Oxford. Bath and Bristol proceeded through Kiln Green, Hare Hatch and Twyford. They crossed the Lodden River, and trotted smartly the five miles on to Reading.

In the 1820s Reading was a pleasant small market town. In its past it could have boasted of one of the greatest abbeys in England, founded by Henry I in 1112 and consecrated by Thomas à Becket in 1164. Ranking after Westminster and Glastonbury it was dissolved by Henry VIII in 1537. The effect of this on the town was disastrous.

Two centuries later it was a great occasion when they held their annual huge cheese fair there. Factors from the west and dealers from London arrived some days before the actual fair day, and until the last moment huge waggons laden with cheeses trundled into the town. Piles of cheeses up to four or five feet high were placed in rows and the narrow walks between were lined with straw. By the end of the day all had disappeared, the cheeses sold and the crowds dispersed.

Reading could provide four hostelries where fresh horses could be obtained. The Bear, the George, the Crown and the Ship, but the Mails called at the Mail Office in Albion Street at a quarter to one in the morning.

The Bath road climbs fairly steeply out of Reading before it enters upon a level stretch running for some miles.

It passed near Calcot Park which in the time of Queen Anne was the home of Sir W. Kendick. Upon his death his only daughter, Frances, inherited his considerable fortunes. As she was reputed to be extremely beautiful she found no shortage of suitors, but in vain did they press their claims, for she had a mind of her own. One day she met casually a young barrister named Benjamin Child at a wedding in Reading. She approved of him and sent an anonymous letter challenging him to a duel or to marry her.

Accompanied by a friend Mr. Child proceeded to the rendezvous which turned out to be in Calcot Park, and there they were met by a masked lady with a rapier in her hand. She informed the gentleman that she was the challenger, and asked Benjamin if he would marry her. Unable to identify her, he requested that she should remove her mask but she curtly refused. He decided in favour of marriage and at the ceremony discovered his bride was indeed beautiful and wealthy. It was recorded to be "a happy marriage" marred by the early death of Frances at the age of thirty-five. Benjamin then sold the house and lived for many years in a cottage in the park. On his death he was buried in the same vault as his wife in the church of St. Mary's, Reading.

The Bath and Bristol Mails hurried through Theale and on towards Woolhampton along the road which still follows the course of the Kennet River flowing slowly between banks lined with reeds and rushes. Just before reaching Woolhampton the Kennet and Avon canal can clearly be seen on the south side of this road. In recent years considerable work has been carried out by enthusiastic volunteers to restore sections of this canal.

About 1810 the stretch between Bath and Newbury was completed so that the distance from Reading to Bristol, some eighty-six miles in extent, became an important inland waterway. From Reading to London the Thames was navigable with the result that heavy loads could be moved by canal and river instead of the 400 miles trip a boat had to make sailing from Bristol via Lands End and the English Channel to London. Obviously the construction was a considerable feat of engineering.

Some coaches called at the Angel and some the Rising Sun at Woolhampton, which was just over ten miles from Reading. Others preferred to drive the extra miles to the King's Head at Thatcham, resulting in a twelve mile stage from there to Hungerford. The inn holder at Thatcham was one of the five enterprising gentlemen who in 1784 entered into an agreement with John Palmer to horse the experimental Mail coach between London and Bristol.

The Mail reached Hungerford at twenty-five minutes past three in the morning. The town of Hungerford is shaped like a letter "T" with the Bath road crossing the main street at the top. The other road leads to Salisbury.

This town has long been famous for fishing and on the Tuesday after Easter the Hock-day celebrations mark the award to the town of these rights by John of Gaunt in the 14th century. "Tuttimen" carrying poles decorated with tutties, or nosegays of flowers, pass from house to house and kiss all the pretty girls after which they assemble to drink the toast to John of Gaunt in a powerful punch.

After changing horses at the Bear, the coach took the new road to Marlborough, which was a great improvement on the twisting lane which wound its way beside the Kennet River to Ramsbury. They drove through Foxfield and climbed gently up through part of the once great forest of Savernake. This was the hunting ground of kings, full of giant beech and ancient oaks. Before actually reaching Marlborough itself the new road descends steeply down Forest Hill. On the London journey they used as many as eight horses to get the coach up the hill. Slowly but safely they made their way into Marlborough with its very wide High Street. As mentioned earlier in regard to Blandford, there had been a number of disastrous fires in the 17th century, so in Marlborough it became an indictable offence to roof with thatch. The Mail proceeded straight up the High Street to stop at the Angel Coach Office for a change of horses. Further on was the Castle Inn where they claimed they horsed up to forty-two stage coaches and carriages a day, and had on this road entertained the best society in the land. Marlborough College is established in part of this building.

To the west there is another hill out of the town, and the road then crosses the Marlborough Downs through Fyfield and West Kennett past farms and cottages constructed of flint, brick and thatch. Even some of the farmyard walls are thatched. Dickens describes this road in *Pickwick Papers* as "a miry and sloppy road, a pelting fall of heavy rain" and a wind that:

> . . . . would come rushing over the hill-tops, and sweeping along the plain, gathering sound and strength as it drew nearer, until it dashed with a heavy gust against horse and man, driving sharp rain into their ears, and its cold damp breath into their very bones.

At Beckhampton the road divides. The Bristol Mail took the top road through Cherhill and Calne, while the Bath Mail took the lower through Devizes and Melksham. The lower road first passes Three Barrows and on to the turnpike gate at Shepherds Shore, erected as early as 1706. Then about a mile further on there is a turning to Bishops Cannings and All Cannings. It was in one of these villages that legend tells how the villagers were caught by customs men in the act of raking the bed of the stream in which the reflection of a great harvest moon was shining. They were asked what they were doing, to which came the reply: "We be trying to rake that there cheese out of the water." The customs men went on their way laughing at these ideas, but the last laugh, however, was with the smugglers. They were actually raking the stream for kegs of gin and brandy which were hidden there. Only their quick thinking and stupid reply put off the customs men.

In those times there was a considerable trade in smuggled Holland gin, brandy and tobacco, much of which found its way to places like Reading and Swindon.

Descending from the Downs the road crosses the Kennet and Avon canal and into Devizes. The change here was at the Black Bear (now the Bear) standing on the south side of the large market square. The time of arrival was six o'clock in the morning; the distance eighty-eight miles from Hyde Park Corner. In about 1775 the landlord of this inn was proud to be able to show to his guests the ability of his six-year-old son in sketching portraits. The boy was Thomas Lawrence, who became one of the most fashionable portrait painters of his time, and eventually President of the Royal Academy.

It is only seven miles from Devizes to Melksham, which was the last change before Bath, and the King's Arms there still exists. The route to Bath did not join the Chippenham road until Bathford was reached. Then they made their way into the city at just before eight o'clock in the morning to the York House at the top of Broad Street. For passengers continuing to Exeter a chance for breakfast.

Bath was an elegant city then, yet in the early 18th century it had been described as a medieval slum. Three men had brought about the improvement. First came Richard Nash. He arrived in the city in 1705, a man of humble background, who had decided to make money quickly so he would have time to enjoy it. When he arrived what he saw horrified him. With his love for order, cleanliness and general decency, he determined that matters had to change in Bath. The streets must be cleaned and paved, the approach roads to the city made passable. This was done. They must have a pump room where the waters could be taken. Dr. William Oliver, who devised the recipe for the Bath Oliver biscuit, helped Nash to organise the raising of funds for the building of the first pump room.

They must have entertainment good enough to attract the best of society. Gradually Nash was able to organise concerts at either Harrison's or Lindsay's Rooms, at which the local gentry could rub shoulders with the best of London society, who were there to take the waters. A great opportunity for a father with marriageable daughters!

In 1720 young Ralph Allen came to Bath as Deputy Postmaster. His grandmother had been Postmistress at St. Columb in the county of Cornwall. He found the postal organisation appalling and set about the task of reorganisation. By sheer luck he obtained news of a Jacobite rising of rebels in the west of England, so he informed General Wade who at that time had his headquarters in Bath. As a result, the general was pleased to give his daughter's hand in marriage to Ralph Allen, and her dowry and social advantages helped this promising young man on the road to success.

Using his wife's money as financial backing Allen improved the Bye-way and Cross-road postal service to everyone's advantage and not the least to the improvement of his own fortunes.

It was John Wood, a young surveyor and builder, who became the third influence in the transition of this city. He had arrived in Bath in 1727 already indoctrinated with the influence of the Palladian style, an interpretation of the classical Roman principles of architecture. What could be more fitting in Roman *Aquae Sulis*?

These three men together helped to realise a dream, Nash in the social sense, Allen and Wood in the material sense, to bring the city to the position it holds today. It is difficult to say how much they worked together towards the ultimate success of their efforts but their achievements are here for all of us to see. Not the least of these being Ralph Allen's house, Prior Park, built by John Wood. However, it is Queen's Square which is John Wood's masterpiece.

*A curricle in the
Crescent, Bath*

By 1764 they were all dead, but the trend of rebuilding in the city was now well established. John Wood, the younger, built the Circus from his father's designs. Then followed the Royal Crescent, the new Assembly Rooms, the Guildhall (built by Thomas Baldwin) and Pulteney Bridge (by Robert Adam). The famous of the land stayed there and were entertained while fashion and snobbery excelled. Bath was without any doubt Sheridan's *School for Scandal*.

The Mail coach was now bound for Exeter by way of Wells so it proceeded down Southgate Street, over the River Avon, and up the long steep hill out of the city. They must have used extra horses here, and at times perhaps some of the passengers may have had to walk for a while.

First through Dunkerton across the Somerset Coal Canal and three miles on to Radstock. Here on the top of the Mendips the land is a large plateau, bare and lonely, a windy place with flat green fields enclosed by long walls of mortarless grey stone, and as one crosses this tableland all is sky.

The old Down Inn still stands at the crossroads of the Bristol to Shepton Mallet and Wells to Bath routes. Here they used to stable between thirty to forty horses.

It is only six miles to Wells. As the coach descended from West Horrington, the outsiders would be able to enjoy a view of this perfect setting, a picture unchanged through several centuries. The triple towers of the cathedral, the palace, cloister and chapter houses, the Deanery and houses of the Close, and the beautiful tower of the parish church blended together to give them their first impressions of the city.

It was a quarter to eleven when the Bath/Exeter Mail passed the Swan, which faces the spacious green and magnificent West Front of the cathedral. It then turned in to High Street to stop at the Somerset Hotel.

Inside the cathedral the nave is evidence indeed of the time when the English builders were enjoying working in the newly developed Gothic style. The unusual but also beautiful inverted arches were inserted when the tower was built in the 14th century. This was the greatest period of architectural activity at Wells, and thus are recorded here the whole range of medieval styles each in harmony with the other. The cathedral of St. Andrew is also rich in its ancient ecclesiastical buildings, as fortunately it has escaped the attentions of the despoilers who have, from time to time, in England's history, defaced and destroyed so much.

The history of Wells is that of the cathedral and they have lived in harmony with each other. They have also shared the Penniless Porch, where beggars used to solicit alms, as a passage between the market place of the city and the sacred ground of the cathedral.

The road from Wells to Glastonbury is flat, surrounded for the most part by level meadows stretching for miles. Ahead is a single conical mound – Glastonbury Tor – over 500 feet high, and surmounted by a 14th century chapel dedicated to St. Michael, which is the last of a number of chapels on this site. From many parts of the Mendips, from all over Avalon and Sedgmoor, from parts of the distant Brendons and Quantocks, one can see Glastonbury Tor. It is a focal point in a very extensive landscape.

First through the Hartlake turnpike (a stone now marks the place) and then over Hartlake bridge, and on this easy ground the horses drew the coach quickly to Glastonbury. They would have passed the ancient frontage of the 15th century Pilgrims Inn, now known as the George. From the top of the coach a good view could be obtained of the ruins of the abbey. Most spectacular was that part of the piers of the crossing, but one could also see the smaller ruined buildings of St. Mary's Chapel and the Abbot's Kitchen.

In 1184 the Norman Abbey was destroyed by fire and rebuilding commenced soon after. Although this great church was completed by 1334, additions and improvements were still being made at the beginning of the 16th century.

So vast and powerful was the abbey it was said of those days that if the Abbot of Glastonbury had been able to marry the Abbess of Shaftesbury, an heir would have inherited more land and more wealth than the King of England owned himself. It is little wonder if this were true that Henry VIII was eager to dissolve these great religious houses.

The last chapters of the glory of Glastonbury were violent. In November, 1538 the aged Abbot Whiting was tied to a hurdle, drawn up the steep slopes of the Tor, and there hanged with two of his monks.

The fate of the abbey, the most ancient in England, was to be stripped of its riches, its fabric gradually reduced to ruins, its vast estates split up and its influence over much of Somerset removed.

The coaches now passed through Walton and Street bound for Pipers Inn. The inn still stands, now just a country pub, the bustle and activity of its former coaching days entirely forgotten.

The road to Bridgwater runs across the Polden ridge. It was started by the Romans, and although at best it is only just over 300 feet high, it commands excellent views on either side. To the north the whole range of the Mendips and Glastonbury Tor, to the south High Ham and Dundon Hill, with the Brendons and Quantocks in the background. This vast expanse of sky would have pleased the artist Constable. In the 12th century much of the land between these hills and the Mendips, known sometimes as Avalon, was flooded to such an extent that a boat could reach Glastonbury.

A gradual descent from the hills, just over two miles before Bridgwater is reached. The road here crosses the western edge of Sedgmoor, and from here into the distance are lush meadows where cattle graze all the summer. There are willows and alders and rhines full of water reflecting the sky. All is peace, yet it was here not more than a few miles away on a misty July night in 1685 that Monmouth's men did battle with the army of the king. The steadiness of the Foot Guards, the ruthless charge of the Life Guards and Blues, cut the peasant army to pieces and settled the matter in an hour and a half, as the records in Westonzoyland church confirm. But the tragedy continued for weeks in trials, executions and transportation, whereas the horror is remembered until this very day.

Bridgwater. The name of this ancient town is derived from Walter's Bridge or Bridge of Walter. It was during the Civil War, which like Taunton saw its fortunes change, that one of its sons obtained fame in Cromwell's service. Robert Blake, born in 1598 and christened in the church of St. Mary's, was the son of a wealthy merchant. He spent some time at Oxford before taking over the family business on the death of his father. He was known to be a religious man of great courage, an able leader and administrator. No doubt for these qualities Cromwell made him his Admiral. He served the Protector well and died as a result of wounds received at a battle with the Spaniards off Santa Cruz.

The Exeter Mail entered Bridgwater by way of East Gate, crossed the bridge over the River Parrett and rattled up Fore Street to stop at the Crown in Cornhill. Both the Crown, and the Angel, which then stood at the rear of this building, were pulled down when the present Royal Clarence was erected on the site.

The up and down Mails arrived here at the same time resulting in great activity. Waiters ready to serve dinner to the passengers; ostlers to change the horses. Some mail to be unloaded, and other bags of mail to be loaded. Way-bills checked. A change of coachmen. There were always some Bridgwater townsfolk with time to watch, and as always the children enjoyed the excitement.

As the time approached for their departure small groups of well-wishers would gather around the respective coaches to say farewell to a friend or relative. Some would ply them with messages for a person in a distant town or city. Guards called for the passengers not yet on the coach. Coachmen took up their seats on the box. Ostlers held the excited horses.

At a quarter past one the Mail coaches left, one bound for London via Bath, and the other for Exeter. A cheer from the crowd as they briskly trotted off in their different directions.

As the Exeter coach proceeded along the Taunton road, the outsiders would have obtained extensive views of Sedgmoor. Few of them possibly realised that it was here in 878, after a strong Danish attack on Wessex, that King Alfred and the West Saxons were driven back to the southern edge of the Mendips. In those days most of Sedgmoor, Mark Moor and Wedmore were flooded in the winter to such an extent that they were an inland sea. Even in summer much was morass and bog. Athelney was but two acres of dry land and Alfred stayed there in hiding for a while before setting forth to harry the Danes. Finally they were beaten in battle and Alfred as king founded an abbey there, but no trace of it exists today.

At Taunton there were three important inns, the Castle, the George and the London Inn (now the County Hotel). The Post Office was at this time in Hammet Street, and Mails changed at the Castle. The Exeter Mail arrived at half-past two.

Towards the close of the 15th century, Taunton was a very prosperous town, which at that time produced one quarter of the country's woollen goods. This prosperity was extended towards the building and improving of their parish church. Some gave generously in their lives, others more generously in their wills. The result was the tower of the church of St. Mary Magdalene, rising to over 160 feet and built of red and golden sandstone.

This tower has dominated the town for four and a half centuries. It looked down during the Civil War and watched the ever changing fortunes of the people as the town was taken and re-taken by both sides. Eventually under Blake the town stood for Parliament, and after some months Fairfax fought off the Royalist besiegers and gave the town peace.

To a community based on trade and valuing this asset, it seems ironical now that the people of this town allowed themselves to be persuaded to proclaim in their market place Monmouth as their rightful king. Several generations had to pay for this indiscretion.

So on towards Exeter, the route taken by the Mail coach was past the George and at the top of High Street they turned for Bishops Hull. An easy climb to this village for a fresh team.

Between here and Wellington there lies to the south the long ridge of the Blackdown Hills, and at the western end stands the Wellington Monument silhouetted against the sky. Although the famous duke took his title from the town, he had little to do with it in reality.

In Wellington the Mails changed horse at the White Hart. The up road to Taunton was an easy stage, the down to Cullompton hard going. Through Rockwell Green and down to Beam Bridge, then up the long hill to Maiden Down and Red Ball would tire the best of horses. Not until Willand was reached could they look forward to an easy run through the Culm valley to Cullompton.

With the modern by-pass, Cullompton has reverted to its former role of a small peaceful town, and one gets the impression that people might not be very surprised if today the Mail coach trotted up the main street to change horses at the White Hart. The present landlords of the inn, however, might find it difficult to produce a fresh team! Although modern shop fronts have replaced the old ground floors, much of this town's skyline can boast of at least one century. The Parish church of St. Andrew is older and one of the finest churches in the county of Devon. Although at one time Cromwell's men stabled their horses in the crypt, fortunately they did little permanent damage to the wonderful rood screen erected about 1450. Apart from a fine roof in the nave and choir, the outstanding feature of this church is the elegant vaulted roof of the south aisle, built in 1526 as the gift of a successful woollen stapler in the town.

There is a distinct similarity in the scenery between the valleys of the Otter, Clyst and Culm. One knows one is in East Devon. Small, friendly villages of cob and thatch. Meadows and orchards. Small farms and cider.

The village of Broadclyst is about seven miles from Cullompton, and as the coach passed through, doubtless some would have noticed the splendid tower of its parish church.

The coach hurried on through Whipton, then a village, to St. Sidwells and the New London Inn in Exeter, to arrive at eighteen minutes past six in the evening, and this completed its journey of 187 miles.

To those passengers who had travelled all the way a tiring journey of just over twenty-two hours. They may, however, have felt that their reward lay in the memories of the varied scenery and the history of the various places through which they had travelled.

5 The Bristol Mail

Travelling by way of Calne, Chippenham and Bath (starting at Beckhampton)

It may have been the inn at Beckhampton called the Waggon and Horses to which Dickens referred after giving his graphic description of the lot of an outsider when crossing the Marlborough Downs. However, the Bristol Mail did not pause to sample its hospitality but drove straight on for Cherill and Calne.

Still the road runs over exposed downland, bleak and uninviting, and not until about a mile from Cherill does the long descent begin. On the south side of the road there is cut in the downland chalk a figure of a horse. About 1780 a Dr. Alsop from Calne arranged the whole business, and it is said he stood about a mile from the workmen who were cutting out the figure shouting instructions to them through a megaphone.

It was also on this stretch of road, according to a Bristol newspaper of March, 1828, that a boy named Emery of Calne was killed. Though there were usually a row of spikes behind both post-chaise and carriages to prevent boys clinging to the rear of the vehicles for an unofficial ride, this did not always discourage them. The lad was young, only seven years old, and saw no danger. Unfortunately when he jumped off it was right into the path of an oncoming Mail coach.

The Mail approached Calne. First it passed the White Hart, then down a short hill to the Strand, which is the old market place of the town. Here stood the Catherine Wheel known to post-boys and coachmen alike as just the Wheel. It existed in the late 16th century but it was the popularity of Bath in the middle of the 18th century which necessitated its enlargement. The Quality stayed here, and here the Bristol Mails changed horse. Sometime in the last century it changed its name to the Lansdowne Arms in honour of the Marquis of Lansdowne, who lived at Bowood House not far from the town. After leaving the inn they drove up the short hill past the King's Arms, where still on the sides of the old coach archway are the notices concerning coaches which used to call there. One side proudly proclaims that "the Eclipse Coach left this office for London every morning at half-past eight o'clock, except Sundays".

The route ahead was by way of Studley and Derry Hill to Chippenham. Here the ostlers at the White Hart had the fresh team ready for the coach expected to arrive at six o'clock.

About four miles north of this town is the village of Langley Burrell. In the 15th century Maud Heath lived here and on her death in 1474 she left sufficient money to build a stone causeway from the village to Chippenham, so that future generations could walk on a dry path instead of the boggy track she had to use to get to market.

From Chippenham an easy road towards Corsham Park and then the Bath road passes between the three villages of Pickwick. There was at this time a Mr. Pickwick who owned the White Hart in Bath, and doubtless he and his family had originated from this area. Further it is believed that Dickens took the name of Pickwick from one of these sources.

Along the side of Box Hill and slowly the coach made its descent to the turnpike gate at the bottom, not far from the present entrance to Box Tunnel. One could not have expected the coachmen and guards working this ground to have heard of Isambard Kingdom Brunel, yet in the early part of 1828 he was convalescing in Clifton after a serious accident in the construction of the Rotherhithe Tunnel. He enjoyed sketching and painting the Avon Gorge, and the idea of a single span bridge across it attracted him as he felt that such a construction would in no way conflict with the grandeur of the scenery but rather it might even enhance it. In spite of the fact that the span exceeded 700 feet across, he submitted plans for the scheme. These were rejected at the time, perhaps because the famous engineer, Telford, categorically stated it was not possible to build a single span which exceeded 600 feet.

Acceptance came for Brunel's plans many years later, but it was too late for him to see it in his lifetime. There were, however, other dreams; a steam railway from London to Bristol, and this he saw accomplished in June, 1841. The projected line of the railway crossed Box Hill, so either he had to make a considerable detour or tunnel through it. Such a tunnel would have to be two miles in length and was at the time considered impossible. Not for Brunel. It was a story of great achievement at great cost. Work began in 1836 and was not completed until 1841. It is estimated it cost well over a million pounds, a huge sum for those days, and it cost the lives of over a hundred men and many more injured.

The brick lining of the tunnel accounted for over thirty million bricks which were brought from Chippenham. No expense was spared in the magnificent portals of the tunnel and no-one will ever know how many tallow candles were used in the digging. This was the price of bringing the railway to Bath and Bristol, but there was another side of the coin. The coachmen, guards, ostlers and inn holders on the Bath road would have to find different employment. There were thousands of them and they knew no skills other than the trade of coaching. And then there was no dole!

About half a mile short of Batheaston the road from Devizes over Kings Down joined the Chippenham road. The lower one was used by the Bath/Exeter Mail, and although only about a mile longer the Bath Mail was some miles from this junction when the faster Bristol coach passed it.

Another turnpike gate at Walcott and another post horn call, and doubtless another gatekeeper wishing the Mails had to stop to pay toll. It would give him more time as he usually waited for stage and carriage to halt in front of the closed gate before he even stirred. Also the Mails travelling through the night passed at most inconvenient times here, about a quarter past seven in the morning, summer and winter, whatever the weather.

Three miles to what was then architecturally the very modern city of Bath. The Bristol coach stopped at the York House, now the Royal York Hotel, at half-past seven in the morning, having covered the 105 miles from Hyde Park Corner in eleven hours. Here in the autumn of 1777, several influential gentlemen from the city and district met and formed a "Society for the encouragement of Agriculture, Arts, Manufacture and Commerce in the counties of Somerset, Wilts., Glos. and Dorset, and the city and county of Bristol." The idea of a Mr. Edmund Rack, who came from Norfolk, it was known as the Bath and West of England Society and is now the Royal Bath and West of England Agricultural Society.

A change of horse and the Mail coach proceeded down Broad Street, where the Post Office was situated at the time, and then through High Street giving any outsiders their first real sight of Bath Abbey church. In those days the houses in Cheap Street continued along the north side of the abbey which restricted the excellent view enjoyed today. This was the church which, when Elizabeth I visited the city on her western progress, caused her such distress as it stood roofless and decaying. She granted Royal Letters Patent ordering collections to be made in all churches annually for seven years to provide for its restoration. The outstanding feature of this church is the superb fan vaulting of both nave and choir, seen to such good effect with the wealth of light penetrating the large perpendicular windows.

Then the coach left the city by way of Stall Street passing the White Hart, down Southgate Street to Bath Bridge. After crossing the Avon it turned westwards towards Twiverton, known as Twerton today.

This stretch of road from Bath to Bristol was considered to be the best in the country at the time, due to the work of John Loudon MacAdam. A Lowland Scot by birth, he came south and lived in Bristol from about 1803. In 1815 he became General Surveyor of the Bristol Turnpike Trust, and he and his sons were advisers to many other trusts in the country. MacAdam understood the principles of good road building, part of which lay in the use of camber. So traffic made good time to Keynsham, an uninteresting place whose abbey Henry VIII dissolved and gave the manor to the wife who survived him, Catherine Parr. This was a busy road and as the Mail hurried westwards heavy lumbering waggons and stagecoaches would pull to one side to let it pass.

Now only five miles to the city and port of Bristol where the coach was due just after nine o'clock in the morning. The old city of Bristol grew up in the small peninsula formed by the junction of the Rivers Frome and Avon. The estuary of the Avon, by a freak of geographical position, does not silt and is subject to very considerable tides. So even before William the Conqueror crossed the Channel, the port of Bristol was established. From the point of view of trade, its position was ideal but from the point of view of defence in times of invasion its position was less satisfactory. So it was in early Norman times a strong castle was built here.

In the reign of Stephen, Bristol became involved in the Empress Matilda's claim to the throne. She was the daughter of Henry I who married the Emperor of Germany and considered her rights stronger than Stephen, and indeed it could be argued they were. After the battle of Lincoln, King Stephen was imprisoned in Bristol Castle and only released when Robert of Gloucester was captured, and the Empress had to agree to exchange the king for her half brother. Although the civil war between Stephen and the Empress Matilda continued for some years, Bristol was left in peace. This period saw the beginning of the Augustine Abbey, which is now the cathedral.

A century later found Bristol on the side of Simon de Montfort in his struggle for the throne. It cost the city the loss of most of its ships in an engagement in the Severn Estuary, and a year later, in 1265, Prince Edward (later Edward I) visited Bristol to levy a fine of £1,000 on its inhabitants for supporting de Montfort.

Obviously a city of such strategic importance was a vital prize in any national struggle for power so it is no surprise to find Bristol involved in the last chapters of Edward II's endeavours to retain his throne. Once again it was a queen, her knight (Mortimer), and her son as a valuable pawn against the king. They moved on Bristol against the king's friends, the Despensers, one of whom was Constable of the Castle. Both father and son were captured and put to death with great brutality. The next move was the capture of the king himself. First he was imprisoned in Bristol Castle and then at Berkeley, where he also was put to death with dreadful barbarity. Even the Abbot of St. Augustine's politely refused burial of the king's body, implying that the Church was also involved in the ruthless schemes of Isabella and her lover.

The merchants of Bristol, already experienced in the export of manufactured cloth, were far sighted enough in 1497 to co-sponsor Cabot on his voyages from Bristol. Always the citizens of Bristol were more interested in trade rather than war, so when the Civil War started, they supported the cause of Parliament. They did not realise how much the city meant to the king and the Royalist cause, and in July, 1643 it finally fell to their determined efforts to capture it. Two years later, towards the end of August, Cromwell encircled the city and by 10th September, Prince Rupert had surrendered. Although the war smouldered on for many months, it was the loss of Bristol which heralded the beginning of the end of the Royalist cause.

Once the city was free, citizens and merchants returned to their trade with vigour. They imported wine from Portugal, sugar from the West Indies, dried fish from Newfoundland and a few years later tobacco from Virginia and cocoa from Africa and, as always, shipbuilding was a Bristol craft.

The 18th century saw Bristol's trade extend into the slavery business and the supply of a wide range of exports to the American and Caribbean colonies. Even the American War of Independence did not affect their prosperity too badly and there remained until the early days of the last century the remunerative slavery business in spite of Clarkson's great efforts.

Considerable fortunes were made by many. The buildings of the city were improved and in many cases endowed. The citizens took pleasure in music and the arts with a theatre opened in 1766. Twelve years later it was granted a licence by Letters Patent and became the Theatre Royal. Young Mrs. Siddons was in the company for two years and at times the best that London could provide at Drury Lane came to Bristol. Performances were well supported for, according to Defoe, "it was not uncommon to see upwards of 100 carriages in the streets around the theatre".

At one time both the Bath and Bristol Theatres were under the same management, that of John Palmer. The cast played at each theatre on alternate nights and were shuttled to and fro in post-chaise together with their costumes and baggage. Doubtless organising this daily service stood him in good stead when later he established the running of the early Royal Mail coaches.

Robert Southey, who was born in Wine Street, said of his birth-place "I know of no mercantile place so literary". He made his own contributions for he worked in the company of Coleridge and Wordsworth, who over a period of four years paid frequent visits to the city.

The Mail coach by now was approaching the city trotting towards the bridge over the River Avon, and at this stage it was the great church of St. Mary Redcliffe which would catch the eye. The original church had a spire on the tower which together rose to a height of 250 feet. In a violent thunderstorm in 1446, most of it had been destroyed and not replaced until 1872. In contrast to her remarks about the Abbey Church at Bath, Elizabeth I, on the same western progress, is quoted as saying that St. Mary Redcliffe was "the fairest, goodliest and most famous parish church in England". This church is a reminder of the times when great rivalry existed between Bristol on the north side of the Avon and Redcliffe on the south.

*The London Mail
arrives at the
Bush, Bristol*

Then on to Bristol Bridge. Replacing a 13th century structure this fine bridge was completed in 1768. It consisted of three wide and lofty arches with handsome stone balustrades. At all four corners of the bridge were the toll houses also built in the same stone quarried at Courtfield in Monmouthshire. In the early 1820s the toll was discontinued and the toll houses became shops.

After crossing this bridge the Mails drove up the High Street, turned left at the Cross into Corn Street and drew up at the Post Office opposite the Bush (now Lloyds Bank). They were due there at four minutes past nine in the morning. One imagines they were met by many merchants or their clerks to obtain the news from London or maybe a sight of one of the London newspapers, for in 1828 the Mails were still the best source of the latest news from the capital.

The Post Office in Bristol was certainly one of the busiest provincial offices in the country as evidenced by the following list:

BIRMINGHAM	Mail arrives	6.45 a.m.	Departs	7 p.m.
PORTSMOUTH	,,	9 a.m.	,,	4.15 p.m.
LONDON	,,	9.4 a.m.	,,	5.20 p.m.
OXFORD	,,	5.5 p.m.	,,	7 a.m.
WEST MAIL	,,	5.15 p.m.	,,	9.30 a.m.
WELSH MAIL	Mail arrives between 3 and 4 afternoon and departs 35 mins after the arrival of the London mail.			

Also foreign mails were departing monthly to America, the Mediterranean, Madeira and Brazil and weekly to Lisbon, and most European countries.

The Welsh Mail would leave Bristol by way of Westbury, Compton Greenfield to New Passage, then across the River Severn by ferry to Black Rock, and a long journey by way of Cardiff and Swansea to Milford Haven.

There was an announcement in the Bristol Gazette in August, 1829 to this effect:

New Passage Ferry

Across the Severn, nearest and most direct route to Wales
Messrs Walker and Wintle most respectfully announce to their friends and the public that the steam packet now plying is much improved and cross at any state of the tide
Milford Mail and Telegraph Coach cross ferry.
The latter leaves Bush Coach office every Tues. Thurs. and Sat. at 7 a.m. thro' Usk to Abergavenny, where it meets the Brecon and Hereford coaches.

They did not mention that the journey from Bristol to Milford Haven would take over twenty-two hours.

From various inns in the city over 200 coaches arrived and departed daily. Competition was keen for custom and judging by a series of advertisements in the press at this time undercutting was carried to the extreme.

The Royal Mail single fare from London to Bristol was £2.5s. inside and £1 outside.

Clift & Co., Plume of Feathers, Wine St., Bristol, quoted £1.18s. inside and 18s. outside.

Nibbletts, General Coach Office, Broad Street, Bristol, £1.12. inside, 12s. outside, which caused Townsends, Bush Coach Office, to reduce theirs to the same as Nibbletts.

In these advertisements the stagecoach proprietors slanged each other on the poor quality of the standard of service given by their competitors!

The centre of Bristol has changed a great deal in a century and a half, but still sufficient remains to form a good picture of the times when outside the Bush there might be as many as ten coaches at any one time and much the same outside the White Hart and White Lion in Broad Street (now the site of the Grand Hotel).

In Corn Street, All Saints Church still stands opposite the Council House built in 1825, although it is no longer used as such. The old Coffee House adjoins the church at the corner of All Saints Lane, and further down this lane is still the Rummer Tavern, from which the very first Royal Mail left for London in 1784. The Exchange built in the 1740s at a cost of around £50,000 has merely weathered over the years, until recently retaining a weekly corn market, and outside the famous bronze short pillars known as the Nails. A reminder of the Post Office building of coaching times is the stone on one corner of the present building inscribed "OLD POST OFFICE". Christ Church stands at the top of Broad Street and St. John's Gate at the bottom.

Never to return, however, is the clamour and the excitement which existed in Corn Street when the Mails arrived with the news of Trafalgar, Waterloo, the death of a king or the passing of the Reform Act.

6 The Gloucester Mail

Travelling by way of Henley, Oxford, Burford, Frogmill and Cheltenham (starting at Maidenhead)

At just before half-past eleven at night the Gloucester Mail pulled away from the Sun at Maidenhead with a fresh team in harness heading for Henley-on-Thames. They drove to Maidenhead Thicket in the company of the Bath and Bristol coaches before turning right for Hurley, while the other two headed for Reading. At one time the vicars of Hurley were robbed here frequently as they went to and from Maidenhead in the course of their duties. They were actually paid an additional £50 per annum for the inconvenience they suffered!

The coach crossed Appletree Hill, descended to Hurley Bottom, where the Toll House still stands, and then trotted up Remenham Hill. From here the descent was through a wood of beech trees to the bridge built in 1786 over the River Thames. They passed the Red Lion and the church as they made their way up Hart Street to stop at the White Hart. Although the inn has been altered since coaching times the original yard is still retained, overlooked by a fine timber gallery. Once spectators watched cockfighting from here, and no doubt more than one saucy chambermaid shouted down to an ostler below.

Henley is today associated not with brewing, although the brewery still operates, nor with coaching, for they no longer trot up and down Hart Street, but with its own Royal Regatta. It all started with the first Oxford and Cambridge boat race held here in 1829.

After leaving the White Hart at just before half-past twelve in the morning they made their way up to Assington Cross, then on through Nettlebed and across Nuffield Heath. There was an inn here where a change of horse was made before proceeding towards Shillingford and Dorchester. About two miles east of Dorchester the up and down Gloucester Mails passed each other. First the horses sensed the approaching Mail, their ears pricked listening to the sound of other hoofs. Each coachman would watch for the glimmer of the other's lamps and then steady the team, to keep them on their own side of the road. This was only done for another Mail coach, and all other traffic must pull as far off the road as possible. Nothing must delay the Mails.

Doubtless an exchange of greeting as they passed, and then each one made its way on in the darkness.

A quick change at the White Hart at Dorchester, and the Mail continued its journey towards Oxford where it was due at three o'clock in the morning. The road they took was by way of Nuneham Courtney, Sandford and Littlemoor.

They trotted along easily on this road, the silence only broken by

*The Gloucester
Mail crosses the
bridge at
Henley-on-Thames*

the clatter of hoofs, the jingle of the harness and the continuous crunch of the wheels on the gravel. Occasionally the coach would lurch as it passed over a pot-hole, and this served as a reminder to the outsiders that it was prudent to remain awake, however tempting it might be to doze.

Once a coachman had a bishop for his companion on the box seat (whether Oxford or Gloucester the story does not confirm). Suddenly there was a shout from the guard for the coachman to stop, and reluctantly the latter complied, as one of the outsiders had fallen off. In spite of his cassock the bishop descended quite nimbly and followed the guard back to find the person concerned. By the light of a lamp they discovered the unfortunate outsider who had dropped off. As they looked at the body the bishop said, "I fear we will not wake him now. God rest his soul." Hence the saying "to drop off to sleep".

Admirers of Oxford say there is only one way to enter the city. To cross Magdalen Bridge and proceed up the High. This is the way the Gloucester Mail travelled but few, except on a fine moonlight night, were able to appreciate the scene. The bridge was narrow (the present one was not built until 1882), so the coachman was more occupied in handling his team than admiring the fine tower of Magdalen. At the east end of the High, where the present examination rooms now stand, was one of the city's renowned coaching inns, the Angel. Day and night they provided hospitality and fresh horses for travellers going to destinations all over the country. If it were a cold night perhaps there was just time while the team was changed at the Angel for a quick glass of neat brandy. The coaching people referred to it as "a flash of lightning".

Oxford today has forgotten the times when a constant feud existed between the citizens of the town and the members of the university. As long ago as February, 1355, there is recorded one of these encounters. Some members of the university were drinking at the Swyndelstock tavern at the Carfax. They considered the wine served to them was bad, so they complained to the landlord. As to the quality of the wine, no-one can know, but we do know that the host did not agree with the complaint and gave a "stub-born and saucy reply". So the graduates, and their rector, who should have known better, threw their flagons and the remains of bottles at the unfortunate landlord's head. He was not accepting this insult without a fight so he called the citizens to his aid. They rang the bell of St. Martin's, Carfax. A crowd gathered and decided to give battle to those who wore the gown. From these small beginnings the incident developed into a three day running battle with many fatal casualties on both sides. The chancellor of the university complained to the king, with the result that the citizens had some of their liberties confiscated.

So the division between the university and the city continued.

*The Angel Inn,
Oxford – his
lordship's carriage
awaits*

Even as late as 1867 the mayor and proctor had to read the Riot Act in a feud between some labourers and freshmen.

The mail bags for Oxford were discharged. A fresh team was harnessed at the Angel. Perhaps a change of passengers. Everybody back on the coach and they were off. They proceeded up the High, past University College, past the ancient church of St. Mary the Virgin, past the Mitre, and on to the ancient crossroads of the city, the Carfax.

Here stood the church of St. Martin's. Now only the tower remains, with the quarter jacks beside the clock, as in 1896 the church was demolished to widen the road. The narrow lane called Butchers Road became Queen Street.

The coach moved westwards along New Road (built in 1766) to cross the Thames or Isis on its way to Botley.

As they travelled through Oxford perhaps some of the passengers remembered that this city was the headquarters of the king during the Civil War. These were the times when the cobbled yard of the Golden Cross was full of finely dressed cavaliers enjoying the admiration of those who looked down from the gallery.

Illustrious colleges, famous churches, celebrated inns were all parts of the Oxford de Quincey knew as an undergraduate in the early years of the 19th century. It was the Mail coach, however, he remembered with affection in his essay *The Glory of Motion*.

He and his fellow students rode outside not because of the lower price but for "the air, the freedom of prospect, the proximity to the horses, the elevation of the seat and the grandeur of the box seat". There was also just an outside chance of purchasing the opportunity of handling the ribbons. To them, according to de Quincey, the roof of the coach was not "the attic or garret" but the "drawing room" and the box seat the "sofa". For the best outside seats the young gentlemen were prepared to bribe those in the coach yard, both horse keeper and ostlers.

The fresh team kept up a smart pace to Botley, then a hamlet of a few wayside houses, and quickly came to Swinford bridge. The guard sounded his horn as they approached for they paid no toll, although users of this bridge still have to do so today.

The inhabitants of Eynsham were asleep as the coach passed through their small town at about half-past three in the morning, driving on to cover the remaining five miles to Witney.

At just after four o'clock, having now covered sixty-nine miles from Hyde Park Corner, the coach drew up outside the Staple Hall Inn at the corner of Bridge Street. The building, though no longer an inn, still stands today.

The River Windrush had certain sulphur properties in the water which improved the colour of wool washed in it, and this enabled the townspeople to build up an extensive business in blankets.

The Gloucester Mail crossed the river and turned into Mill Street so the passengers were not able to see the Blanket Hall with its one-handed clock built in 1721 or the 17th century Town Hall and still older Butter Cross. They clattered down Mill Street heading for Burford. The road soon starts to climb to the exposed high table-land above the beautiful valley of the Windrush River.

After three miles they passed the turning to Minster Lovell. A long story could be told if all the history of this ancient house and its family were known. Today it stands in ruins, but the Lovell family existed here as early as the 12th century, although not until the Wars of the Roses did they seem to figure in history. Frances Lovell supported first the Lancastrian side but when their fortunes were at a low ebb he became a Yorkist. So he is remembered by a rhyme of the period:

The Cat, the Rat and Lovell the dog,
Rule all England under the Hog.

The Cat was Catesby; the Rat, Radcliffe; and the Hog, Richard III, whose favourite badge was the Blue Boar.

When Henry VII won the throne at Bosworth, Lovell escaped overseas. He returned with Lambert Simnel, fought at the battle of Stoke, and was never seen again. One of the many stories concerning his disappearance was that he was drowned as he tried to escape across the River Trent. Another tells how he returned to Minster Lovell and hid in a secret room known only to his most devoted servant. Here he was locked in with adequate provisions to await the time when he could flee abroad again. Whether his servant died suddenly, or yielded to some form of treachery the story does not relate. What is known, however, is that at the beginning of the 18th century during alterations to the house a hidden room was discovered. Inside was the skeleton of a man seated at a table, while all around were decaying books, empty bottles and bones.

The road starts to climb – the horses sensed this and pulled into their collars – as the Gloucester Mail hurried westwards towards Burford.

With sharp stones on the road horses frequently became lame. In spite of the demands placed on contractors by the Post Office that only sound animals should be used, sometimes a partly lame horse was harnessed in the change especially at night. A few miles work on the road and the horse was then useless. One way or another lame horses were a common problem. When it happened the coachman reined in his team, the guard leapt from the coach and unharnessed the unfortunate animal, possibly to the background of curses from coachman or outsiders. The team had to be reharnessed as one leader and two wheelers. If the unsound horse was a leader it would be a comparatively easy task, but if a wheeler it meant a double change, as one of the leaders had to become a wheeler. The guard knew only too well the importance of keeping time. The tradition of the service demanded this. He must therefore be proficient in this work and at the worst the delay should not exceed two minutes. The three horses were described as being harnessed in unicorn.

The lame animal was let loose. Perhaps horse sense was the deciding factor whether it followed the direction of the coach or returned to the last posting inn. However, horses being horses, the time taken on the journey would depend to a great extent on the quality of the grasses on the roadside!

Today one usually enters Burford to see the attractive High Street descending towards the River Windrush. The Bull Inn still remains as does the Tolsey, which serves as a reminder of the days when the manorial market tolls were still payable here.

The Mails, however, made a more gradual descent to the bottom of the town. They left the present road at White Hill and entered Burford by way of Witney Street. They stopped for breakfast, and at twenty minutes past five picked up any other passengers at Church Green. In midsummer it would be light enough for those waiting here for the coach to gaze at the fine 15th century three-storied porch and south doorway of the Parish Church. They could see the Norman tower capped with the spire added in the 15th century, which at the time caused the builders certain problems in the form of subsidence. In the churchyard could be noticed the curious "wool bale" tombs.

They moved off on time. Past the old Bear Inn, along Sheep Street, to start the climb to Upton Down. From here to Northleach they travelled over a windswept road. In the dark days of winter coachmen huddled deep in their many coats, and outsiders stamped their feet to keep warm to the annoyance of those inside. In Shakespeare's Richard II, Northumberland says about a similar road:

These high wild hills and rough uneven ways
Draw out our miles and make them wearisome.

So they struggled on past the lodge gates to Sherborne Park, past New Barn inn and on towards Northleach.

The town itself was just one long street of stone-built houses, a wonderful 15th century church, renowned for its many fine brasses, two inns and a prison. The prison was built about 1790 by Sir George Paul, who also built Gloucester jail. In his younger days he was a wealthy young man who enjoyed the good life. Later, as a magistrate, he took an interest in penal reform with the result that the two new prisons he built were a great improvement on any other jails in the country.

In the town record book there are entered under a date in 1576 the thirty-nine ordinances of Northleach possibly based on Saxon laws and customs. They include:

> Any apprentice caught in the streets after the ringing of the curfew bell be put in the stocks until morning . . . .

and

> Playing, gaming or dancing during the time of divine service – the offender to be fined 6d.

No doubt with such rules Northleach was a very law abiding place.

The tired horses gave way to a fresh team provided at the Sherborne Arms and the Mail left quickly for Frogmill seven miles nearer Cheltenham.

They climbed steadily up to the Puesdown Inn before starting the long descent past the Old Pike House towards Shipton Oliffe. Approaching the village their road ran alongside a stream with willows growing on the banks. The horses hastened through the twisting road of the village knowing their task was nearly over as the Mail approached Shipton Sollers with its ancient Frogmill mentioned in the Domesday Book.

Until around 1800 this point was the end of the coach run from London and passengers and Mail changed into a post-chaise to complete their journey to Cheltenham and Gloucester. By the late 1820s, however, the road had been improved and more than twenty coaches a day called at Frogmill.

Part of the old inn still remains today and has been incorporated into a modern hotel. The rules of the house which still survive give an insight into the travellers of nearly two centuries ago:

> Fourpence a Night for a Bed:
> Sixpence including Supper.
> No more than THREE to Sleep in a Bed.
> No Ale allowed Upstairs;
> No Smoking in Bed;
> No Boots to be worn in Bed.
> No Dogs or Monkeys Upstairs.
> No Gambling or Fighting.
> No Razor Grinders and the Like
> To Sleep in the Attic.

Here the Gloucester Mail arrived at five minutes past seven in the morning having completed ninety-two miles since leaving Hyde Park Corner.

The road from Frogmill to Charlton Kings descends nearly 500 feet down to the wide fertile Severn valley and from the road there are extensive views stretching to the Forest of Dean and the Malvern Hills.

In 1828 Cheltenham was well served by stagecoaches. Listed in the town's directory are over sixty daily departures to destinations all over the country, departing from the George, Royal, Plough, Golden Lion and Feathers. In addition to these there were many others running on certain days of the week. Few ran on Sunday apart from the Mails.

The Mail called briefly at the Plough and left for Gloucester at twelve minutes to eight. They turned off the Tewkesbury road and headed for Staverton Bridge. By half-past eight they were only two miles from the Wooton turnpike gate, and just three miles from Gloucester itself. At a quarter to nine they would draw up at Heath's coach office.

At half-past eight the Poole Mail was well on its way to Wimborne Minster, while Bath/Exeter, after stopping in Bath for breakfast, was at this time climbing the long hill out of the city on the Wells road. The Devonport Mail, having completed 116 miles of its long journey, was changing horses at Sherborne, while the Bristol Mail was due in that city in half an hour. The Exeter coach had left Blandford and was on its way to Dorchester.

Twelve hours before they had all passed Hyde Park Corner together.

7 The Poole Mail

Travelling by way of Farnham, Alton, Winchester, Southampton, Ringwood and the New Forest (starting at Bagshot)

A quarter of an hour after the Devonport Mail had left the King's Arms at Bagshot, the Exeter and Poole coaches pulled in to change horse. A chance for a quick drink and then they were off. They climbed the hill together to the Jolly Farmer and here they parted, no doubt with good wishes for a safe journey. The Poole coach turned on to the Farnham road and was now alone. This ten mile stretch over Frimley Heath past the White Hart in the village itself and over the Blackwater River to Farnborough would not be recognised by the coaching people if they saw it today. At that time it was just heathland crossed by a lonely road. Guards sat with their blunderbuss on their lap just in case some villain felt disposed to try and rob His Majesty's Mail. After the village of Farnborough came Farnham Heath, and they were still four miles from the Bush in the town itself. By one o'clock they had reached Farnham where the castle is set high above the town. Built in the 12th century, it belonged to the Bishops of Winchester until recent times, and royalty have been entertained here over the centuries.

A quick change of horse and they left for Alton on an easy level road through Bentley Green and drove into Hampshire. Here the up and down Mails passed. The London coach was due at the Bush at a quarter to two and reached the General Post Office in London at six twenty later that morning. Such was the accuracy of their timing that they passed every night at almost the same place, and should one perhaps be a minute or so late doubtless some comment was made when eventually they passed. This was a great moment on the stage but an anti-climax. The excitement of anticipation, the passing and then the routine of the journey.

The Poole coach continued its journey through Froyle and Holybourne to arrive at the Crown at Alton at ten minutes past two. In this town Sir William Waller attacked and routed Lord Crawford after the Royalist peer had failed to fulfil his promise of swapping with the Roundheads a fat ox for a cask of wine!

Seven minutes after leaving Alton the coach trotted quickly through the village of Chawton and turned the corner past the house which was once the home of Jane Austen. The property is now a museum in the care of the Jane Austen Memorial Trust. In this house, surrounded by so much that this lady knew and cared about, one can look out of a window facing the Winchester road and imagine the sound of the Mails as they passed each night. The up Mail at twenty-three minutes after midnight, the down at seventeen minutes past two in the morning.

76

*The up and down
Mails pass near
Farnham*

She wrote of the house in a letter to her brother, Captain Francis Austen (who later became Admiral of the Fleet):

Our Chawton Home, how much we find
Already in it to our mind:
And how convinced, that when complete
It will all other houses beat
That ever have been made or mended,
With rooms concise or rooms distended.

In the room where she did most of her literary work, the door still creaks. She appreciated the value of this because she did not wish either visitors or servants who might interrupt her to discover the secret of her authorship. While she lived here she saw published those books originally written at Steventon; *Pride and Prejudice*, *Sense and Sensibility* and *Northanger Abbey*. Actually written in the house were *Mansfield Park*, *Emma* and, although then failing in health, her last novel *Persuasion*. In 1816 she went to lodge in North Street, Winchester, to be near her physician. The following year she died and was buried in Winchester Cathedral, not on account of her fame at this time but because her death took place in the parish.

In summer and winter it was always dark or at the best moon-light as the Mails drove the remaining nine miles to Alresford, travelling by way of North Street, Ropley Dean and Bishops Sutton. Both then and now most travellers to this town only know the main street of New Alresford in which the Bell and the Swan still stand. The charm of Alresford really exists in Broad Street with its Georgian houses, old Fulling mill and lime trees.

At ten minutes past four with a fresh team harnessed to the coach they moved off from the warmth and comfort of the Swan to proceed towards Winchester. The guard broke the silence of the night as he sounded his horn to warn the keeper of the turnpike gate at Staple Green of the approach of the Royal Mail.

To the east of this road lies Tichborne. Here in 1150 as Lady Marbella Tichborne lay dying, she requested her avaricious husband to use some of his many acres to grow corn for the poor. She had all her life shown concern for those in need. As he considered her to be too ill to even leave her bed he agreed to her request on the condition that he would set aside for this purpose as much land as she could walk around while a brand taken from the fire continued to burn. Legend says she managed to crawl around some twenty acres and as she died pronounced a curse upon the house if ever this dole should be discontinued. The land concerned is known as the Crawls. In 1796 the dole was changed to a gift for the church and some years after troubles started for the family with Roger, the sole heir, reported to have been lost at sea. Although his mother still believed him to be alive, the direct line of succession seemed doomed to extinction. In about 1870 a certain butcher from Australia who must have met people who knew this Roger, came to England to claim the title. Even Roger's mother believed, or wished to believe, this butcher was in fact her son. His claim, however, was contested by certain relatives and in 1871 a long and sensational court case followed. Finally the butcher was exposed as a fraud and sentenced to fourteen years imprisonment. The dole, now of flour, is still distributed to the villagers on the 25th of March each year.

The passengers, cramped in the stuffy interior of the coach, who might have felt like a doze on this stage of the journey, would have been awakened again as the guard alerted the keeper of the Shortledge Gate. Not long after this they descended Magdalen Hill, crossed the bridge over the Itchen River and rattled over the cobbles as they proceeded up the High Street of the city of Winchester, the ancient capital of England and still older capital of Saxon Wessex.

In its formidable Norman castle King Stephen imprisoned his cousin the Empress Matilda but she escaped hidden in a coffin. It suffered badly during the Civil War but the Great Hall is still in existence together with its famous Round Table. Until the late 14th century Parliament met here when assembled in this city.

The great cathedral started by the Normans to replace an earlier Saxon building took nearly 500 years to build in its entirety. The twelve bays of the beautiful Gothic nave, which is the largest in the world, are the work of William of Wykeham and his master mason William Wynford in the late 14th century. William Wykeham, who was without doubt the greatest of the bishops of this diocese, was also the founder of Winchester College. His tomb, in a chantry in the Nave, was situated where, according to legend, as a boy he listened to the services and decided to devote his life to the church. Delicate Gothic and austere Norman blend well within the confines of this immense building. Norman and Plantaganet kings lodged frequently in the city as they journeyed from London to their French domains. Henry VII, always anxious to establish his family as one of ancient lineage, arranged for his eldest son, Arthur, to be christened in the cathedral. Sadly Charles I's last visit to the city was as a prisoner in 1648.

Royalty and the Church feature much in Winchester's long history.

From Wells and Caigers' coach house which stood in the High Street the Poole Mail left on the Southampton stage at ten minutes past four in the morning. It turned into Southgate Street and moved quickly down St. Cross road. In the right circumstances those outside would obtain a glimpse of the Hospital of St. Cross which was founded by Henry de Blois, a grandson of William the

Conqueror some 850 years ago. He conceived the idea of building a charitable institution to house thirteen poor men, and it is still a home for pensioners. Some wear black gowns with a silver cross of Jerusalem and medieval caps while those from the almshouses of the Noble Poverty (founded in 1445 by Cardinal Beaufort) wear claret coloured gowns, caps and a cardinal's badge. Their Norman chapel must be one of the finest churches of this period in the country today. Of course no passenger was able to stop and sample the custom of the Wayfarers' Dole, which dates from the 12th century. It consists of a gift of bread and ale served in a horn, which is still granted to poor travellers today.

From Winchester two roads lead to Southampton. The western road runs via Otterborne and Chandlers Ford. The eastern one through the Itchen valley. The Mails take the former road which follows the even older Roman one part of the way. They passed through Chandlers Ford and Cranby Park where Sir Isaac Newton spent the last years of his life with his adopted daughter and her husband. They pressed on to Southampton. The Norman Conquest brought about the early development of this city as it was the natural port for communication between Normandy and Winchester. The town was built on a grid pattern within its strong walls of defence and the main street (now High Street) was once referred to as English Street while parallel to it was French Street. The Middle Ages saw a decline in its importance with the loss of the French possessions but it was from here that the Pilgrim Fathers set sail for America. One of their two ships, the *Speedwell*, was not seaworthy so they had to put in to Plymouth and then all embarked in the *Mayflower*.

The guard delivered the mail to the General Coach House in Above Bar Street at thirty-five minutes past five o'clock in the morning. A fresh coachman took over, a fresh team provided by Harry Ayles, who was at this time the contractor for the lower ground, Southampton to Poole. The route taken by the coaches was referred to as the "Ground" and divided into the Upper Ground (nearest London), in between the Middle Ground and the section nearest their destination the Lower Ground. They travelled through Redbridge, Totton and Netley Marsh to Cadnam, where they changed to a fresh team before taking the lonely road through the New Forest.

This was one of the eighty forests designated by the Normans. One thinks today of forests as dense wooded areas but really they were regions set aside for the king's pleasure in hunting. Many of the great forests such as Savernake, Cranbourne Chase and Nottingham have dwindled in size but the New Forest is still very much as the Normans knew it at least in extent. It still retains quite a number of their original laws. Over the centuries there was a continual struggle between the monarchs endeavouring to preserve their kingly rights where deer were more important to them than the commoners dwelling there, and it continued until the last century. In 1877 in an Act of Parliament the commoners' rights were defined and the English Court of Verderers was reinstated to see these enforced. Four of these rights were:

The right of grazing for cows, horses and geese.
The right of Mast to graze pigs on acorns and beech mast in the pannage season (25th September to 30th November).
The right of Estover to take wood from forests to be burnt in all houses that carried this right.
The right of Turbary to cut turves for burning on the hearth of those householders entitled to this right.

The Verderers Court continues to sit at Queens House, Lyndhurst, to hear any grievances of the commoners. The members of this court keep law and order within the confines of the forest and to assist them officers called Agisters patrol the forest on horseback.

From Cadnam the road climbs for about two miles through mature woodland and then runs over the high ground of gorse, heather and bracken to Picket Post.

The guards, many of whom had served as soldiers, were referred to in coaching slang as "shooters". It was stages like this one which provided the chance of poaching the odd pheasant, partridge or hare, as they covered this stretch of road between half-past six and half-past seven in the morning. Eventually this indiscretion on the part of some guards came to the notice of the Post Office authorities, causing Hasker to issue an order that "Guards must on no account shoot game".

Guards were allowed tips and they called those passengers who did not give generously enough "scaly" ones. In keeping the Way-bill, on which the number of passengers had to be entered, there was always the temptation to leave one off and pocket the fare. Such passengers were known as "the short one" or "bits of fish". However, the Post Office disciplinary powers were both wide and punitive and kept the majority of guards completely honest.

The letters they carried from London to Southampton cost 8d. and those to Poole 9d.

In many cases people fetched their mail from the town post office, though in Southampton there were local carriers for outlying districts which presumably levied a further cost for this service. When the cost of postage in these times is related to average earnings of between 10s. to 14s. per week, it becomes apparent that only the wealthy could afford the service. The cost of travelling at this time was also expensive. On the Mails around 2d. a mile as an outsider and over 4d. a mile to travel inside.

The rates of postage in 1828 were:

"From any Post Office in England or Wales to any Place not exceeding Fifteen Miles from such Office, 4d.

Above	and not exceeding		Above	and not exceeding	
15 M.		20 M. . . . 5d.	170 M.		230 M. . . . 11d.
20 M.		30 M. . . . 6d.	230 M.		300 M. . . . 12d.
30 M.		50 M. . . . 7d.	300 M.		400 M. . . . 13d.
50 M.		80 M. . . . 8d.	400 M.		500 M. . . . 14d.
80 M.		120 M. . . . 9d.	500 M.		600 M. . . . 15d.
120 M.		170 M. . . . 10d.			

And so increasing One Penny for a Single Letter on every like excess of One Hundred Miles.

Letters to and from Scotland are charged $\frac{1}{2}$d. more than the above Rates.

Note.– No Letter charged more than Treble, unless the same shall weigh an Ounce; then to be rated as four single Letters, and so in proportion for every Quarter of an Ounce. – Letters to Soldiers and Sailors, if single, charged One Penny only."

The coachman was employed by the contractor and his responsibility was just to handle the horses and get the coach safely to the next stage. All other worries, and there could be many, belonged to the guard. He was the custodian of the Mails. Any failure not to mend a broken trace or release a lame horse in reasonable time resulted in a stern rebuke from those in power at the General Post Office.

It seems that the poor unfortunate guard was blamed for everything, as evidenced in the following letter:

> General Post Office,
> 29th July, 1826.
>
> Sir,
> The passengers who travelled with the Portsmouth to Bristol Mail on the 26th instant having complained that the coachman who drove on that day from Bristol to Warminster was drunk, and unfit to drive, I have to desire you will explain the reason why you neglected to report to me so great and so disgraceful an irregularity, and also how it happened that you did not know the coachman's name, when the passenger asked you for it.
> I am, Sir,
> Yours, etc.

It was a long stage of twelve miles from Cadnam to Ringwood, so the tired horses sensed that as they passed Picket Post the road descended gradually down towards Ringwood. Here a chance for some refreshment in the twenty minutes stop at the Crown, and at ten minutes to eight they left for Wimborne Minster.

The road was by way of St. Leonard's Bridge to Tricketts Cross, over Fern Down to Leigh. A landscape then of wild heath land and scrub, now just a straggling line of bungalows, houses, nursery gardens interspersed occasionally with pines and rhododendrons.

They approached the turnpike at Leigh. This scene was so well described by de Quincey:

Look at those turnpike gates, with what deferential hurry, with what an obedient start, they fly open at our approach! Look at that long line of carts and carters ahead, audaciously usurping the very crest of the road. They do not hear us as yet but as soon as the dreadful blast of our horn reaches them with the proclamation of our approach, see with what frenzy of trepidation they fly to their horses' heads.

They drove into the market square of Wimborne; de Quincey again:

Sometimes after breakfast His Majesty's Mails would become frisky; and in the difficult wheelings amongst the intricasies of early markets, it would upset an apple cart, or a cart loaded with eggs! Could the progress of the Royal Mail be expected to be affected by minor accidents of this kind!?

They left the pleasant town of Wimborne dominated by the twin towered minster church of St. Cuthberga and turned south to head through Oakley and over Canford Heath to Fleets Corner. Then before them lay the vast expanse of Poole Harbour with the tang of the sea and the sound of gulls.

The old residents of Poole will tell you that "it was a thriving town when Bournemouth was but furzen down". There is plenty of evidence of its importance in the past in the older part of the town near the harbour quay, with the ancient town cellars and nearby the old lock-up. Its Customs House, rebuilt in 1813 after the previous building had been burnt down, dealt with many cases of smuggling. The Harbour Office, warehouses, and ships chandlers recall the days of its greatest prosperity in trade with Newfoundland in both timber and cod. It is, however, the Guild Hall erected in 1762 which is the outstanding building. Originally the street level was open and used as a market while above it was the Chamber Room and Court House. It is now a most interesting museum.

Smuggling by ordinary people was one thing but smuggling by the guards of the Royal Mail quite another. Obviously the opportunity existed especially from places like Poole, and therefore it comes as no surprise to find that one of the guards of the Poole/Southampton coach was suspected of carrying contraband. The mail box at the rear of the coach had to be kept locked at all times, and customs officers would have to request the key before it could be searched.

His Majesty's guard refused, the officers of His Majesty's Customs persisted. Finally the guard levelled his blunderbuss defying them to touch His Majesty's Mail at their peril, and the Mail drove off.

The matter did not end there; it was followed by a lengthy correspondence between the Postmaster General and the Commissioners of Customs. Neither side ever gave way!

Through Poole's narrow streets the Mail proceeded to complete its long journey at the Antelope. They arrived at a quarter to ten having covered just over 113 miles from Hyde Park Corner in thirteen-and-a-quarter hours.

Yet at half-past four the same afternoon the Poole Mail coach left again for London where it was scheduled to arrive back at the General Post Office at twenty minutes past six the following morning.

PART TWO

From St. Martin's le Grand

8 The Edinburgh Mail

London to York by way of Grantham

By the mid 1820s the General Post Office had outgrown its premises in Lombard Street resulting in considerable congestion in the area at the time of morning arrivals and, even worse, the evening departures. In 1829 the move planned four years previously was made to a fine new two-storied building faced with an Ionic Portico in St. Martin's le Grand. Designed by Sir R. Smirke, R.A., and erected on the site of the old church of St. Martin. Although the Western Mails had left Piccadilly for many years they continued to do so after the move, in spite of the fact the adjoining yards were quite extensive enough to accommodate them.

Opposite the General Post Office, on the west side of the street, Mr. E. Sherman had rebuilt and enlarged his premises, the Bull & Mouth Inn. Completed around 1830 the façade was finished in red brick and Portman stone, and renamed the Queen's Hotel. Custom resisted the change in name and as long as the coaches were running the hotel was always known as the Bull & Mouth. From here about thirty long distance coaches left each day, and it was in a very favourable position to horse a number of the Mails on their first stage out of town. The vast underground stables could house over 400 horses, which necessitated a staff of 200 ostlers and horse keepers, all under the supervision of the yard porter. If favours were required, a problem over luggage, or a young man attempting to obtain the box seat, the yard porter was the person to approach, but he had to be tipped generously.

During the day letters could be handed in at coffee houses and inns chosen for this purpose by the Post Office authorities. After five in the afternoon a bellman collected letters for a further hour receiving a fee of a penny each. The General Post Office accepted letters up to seven in the evening and even until half-past seven if one felt the urgency was worth a "Late Fee" of 6d!

By half-past seven the mail coaches which during the day had been cleaned and overhauled at Vidler's Yard, Millbank, were returned to the Post Office and drawn up in departure order. Post-chaise and coach arrived with passengers who had assembled at various London hostelries. Some argued over the seats, while others fussed over their luggage. Guards checked the passenger lists, watched the luggage stored, and supervised the loading of the mails. Horses were restless, ostlers shouted, street boys and pedlars seeking passengers' attention jostled with porters. All this to the amusement of the crowd peering through the railings.

The passengers booked through to Edinburgh had a journey of 399 miles ahead of them. Of course it was possible to break the journey at a convenient point such as York, get a good night's sleep, and catch the Mail or a stage the next day but it added to the expense.

In the 1830s for an inside seat the fare was £9. 19s. 6d. With the cost of meals and tips added the total was around £12. It would have taken a labourer four months to earn this sum. Outside it was only half the fare but other overheads were the same. If you were escorted by a servant you tipped for him or her as well.

If money was not a vital consideration then the journey to Edinburgh could be done in style, by post-chaise. The cost, at certainly 1s. per mile, plus good accommodation, good food and wine – and a good many tips – could mean an expense of about £35.

At their best the Mails took forty-two-and-a-half hours to complete the journey to the Scottish capital. The achievement of Sir Robert Cary, doubtless with great rewards in view, must remain one of the outstanding journeys in history. The year 1603, the occasion the death of Queen Elizabeth I. Sir Robert left London on the morning of Thursday, 24th March, travelling over roads which were at best rough pack horse tracks, and much of the time in the dark of night, changing horses wherever he could, taking little food or rest, arrived in Edinburgh late Saturday afternoon in just under sixty hours!

The evening exodus of the Mails started at eight o'clock with Edinburgh, Glasgow, Louth and others moving into the street of St. Martin's le Grand, with the dome of St. Paul's as a backcloth to the scene. The noise of so many hooves and wheels on the cobbles must have been deafening.

They soon reached Shoreditch Church, which was the point from which the road to York and Edinburgh was measured. They proceeded up the High Street which in the 1830s was a slum. Even at this time in the evening there was traffic. Heavy waggons drawn by heavy horses slowly making their way to the markets, stages from the north rushing into town, cabs and gigs, post-chaise, and three-horses omnibus, all jostling for the best position of the road. In spite of the work of many street urchins, who collected manure and sold it, the stones were still covered with horse dung. Ragged children watched the passing of the Mails with the appreciation of a good theatre audience. Older people gazed, not excited, but curious. The guards of the two coaches trotting up the street stood resplendent in their red uniforms, full of their importance and missing no opportunity to sound their horns. The notes rang out. "Clear the road" was recognised by all. Even the mongrel dogs sniffing on the highway took heed and escaped from under the leaders' hooves just in time.

The rookeries of Shoreditch gave way to more respectable properties by the time Kingsland Road was reached. According to *Pigot's Directory* in 1836, the Edinburgh coach called at the Cherry

Tree, Kingsland Road, presumably to pick up passengers, but after a century and a half the Cherry Tree has disappeared.

They trotted on towards Stoke Newington, a small town of some three to four thousand inhabitants lodged in houses and above shops along its straggling street. Now they were off the stones and on to a gravel road the clatter of hooves and wheels was quieter and there was less jolting of the coach.

Up Stamford Hill the horses strained. This was where the rich City merchants lived, with a distant view of London churches and St. Paul's. They passed through the turnpike gate, and descended smartly to Tottenham village. On the Green is the High Cross, a wooden column placed there in the Middle Ages and taken down in the early 17th century when the present octagonal column was erected by Dean Wood. The column is built of brick and was given a coat of stucco around 1809.

The Mails moved quickly through Tottenham village and on towards Edmonton. They passed All Saints Church, where Charles Lamb and his sister Mary are buried, and the Bell Inn known later for its association with Cowper's ballad *John Gilpin*.

At eighteen minutes past nine o'clock Waltham Cross was reached. A change of horse and an exchange of mail bags at the Post Office, for in 1836 a cross-post was instituted between Barnet on the Holyhead road and Waltham Cross on the Old North Road. A guide book of the 1830s draws attention to "on the right between 11th and 12th milestone Abbey Church and powder mills", but makes no mention of Eleanor's Cross, yet until the late 18th century the town was known as Eleanor's Cross, Waltham. The cross itself is one of twelve set up by Edward I at the resting places of his wife's body on the long funeral journey from Harby near Lincoln to Westminster Abbey. Only two others remain now, at Geddington and Hardingstone.

The road continues to run parallel to the River Lea through the narrow streets of Cheshunt, then through Broxbourne and Hoddesdon and the Bull Inn to reach the Saracen's Head at Ware. This inn is remembered for once owning the Great Bed of Ware, now in the South Kensington Museum.

They drove down the High Street past a number of 17th century buildings and hurried northwards with the fresh team. Although Puckeridge was only a hamlet it boasted of a post office, so any bags had to be exchanged, but the Mail did not stop.

A change at Buntingford, seven miles to Royston where the Mail arrived at the Red Lion at four minutes past twelve. By now the Louth coach was two miles behind the Edinburgh while the Glasgow travelling along the Great North Road had reached Baldock.

From Royston to Arrington Bridge was referred to as "good galloping ground", which meant the coachman would put the horses into a controlled canter for a while, but they were never galloped except by the reckless. The Mails in particular maintained their speed of ten miles per hour by quick changes and good driving of horses capable of sustaining an extended trot for the whole of the stage. At Arrington Bridge, and Caxton, they changed again, drove past Caxton Gibbet and Kisby's Hut to Godmanchester, a name which sounds as if it comes from a Trollope novel. It was an important Roman posting station at the crossroads of the Via Devana (Colchester to Chester) and Ermine Street (London to York). In spite of its long history there is no High Street or market place, but it still retains a number of fine half-timbered houses.

A certain Thomas Weems of Godmanchester decided to kill his wife and seek his fortune in London. He lured her to a lonely place and murdered her, certainly not expecting the deed to have been witnessed. It was, by a woman tending a sick cow in a field, who rushed to the road. There she stopped a passing coach in which, by pure coincidence, was a Justice of the Peace. She told him her tale, and Weems was apprehended at Royston. He was tried and hanged at Cambridge.

The townsfolk felt that the events leading to his arrest were the result of Divine intervention so subscribed to a fund to erect a tombstone in the churchyard in 1819 which reads:

Ere crime you perpetrate, survey this stone,
Learn hence the God of Justice sleeps not on his throne
But marks the sinner with unerring eye
The suffering victim hears, and makes the guilty die.

The Edinburgh Mail crossed the 14th century bridge over the River Ouse, and trotted into the High Street at Huntingdon. Part of the yard of the George Inn still remains, an open gallery running along one side with a staircase leading from the yard itself. It is believed that the George was owned at one time by Oliver Cromwell's grandfather. Certainly Oliver Cromwell, and later for a short time, Samuel Pepys, attended the grammar school in the town.

They left Huntingdon at fourteen minutes past two in the morning and climbed to the summit of Alconbury Hill, which is only 164 feet high but commands a good view of the surrounding Fens. Here is the junction of the Great North Road (A1) over which the Glasgow Mail ran, and the old North Road (A10 and A14), the route taken by the Edinburgh and Louth Mails. The latter is four miles shorter. At this point stands an old signpost in the form of an obelisk. About 100 yards north was the famous Wheatsheaf (now two private houses) a most important posting house. Both day and night post boys were ready, and the stud of horses maintained here in John Wersop's time was around 100. First to arrive was the Edinburgh Mail at a quarter to three and they expected the Glasgow at one minute before three o'clock. Although these coaches would now travel over the same road as far as Newark, they would still be fourteen minutes apart.

First came the descent of Stangate Hill, and then they trotted in the dark the level road to Stilton. Like all the inns on this road the Bell and the Angel both gave a twenty-four hour service. The Bell, built of a warm mellowed stone, can still be visited, but its imposing gallows sign has disappeared. The Edinburgh Mail arrived at forty-two minutes past three having covered seventy-one miles.

Paterson's Roads, in 1826 quotes:

> Stilton has long been celebrated for the excellence of its cheese not infrequently called the English Parmesan, which was first made by Mrs. Paulet, of Wymondham, Nr. Melton Mowbray, Leicestershire, who supplied the celebrated Cooper Thornhill, Innholder of the Bell, who sold it for 2/6 a lb.

These cheeses were eagerly purchased by travellers for themselves or friends, and for many years the landlord of the Bell kept the secret well. Then Miss Worthington of the Angel opposite began to supply her visitors, and the secret leaked out, but not before the name had become firmly established.

Whether passengers on the Edinburgh Mail were keen to purchase Stilton cheese at this hour of the morning is a matter for conjecture, but the demand was great enough to tempt more than one guard on the up Mail to carry some in his box, to customers he could trust in London, in spite of the fact it was against the Post Office regulations. At least it did not smell as much as fresh fish – which some guards carried on parts of their journey.

A mile after Stilton is the turning for Peterborough at Norman Cross. Here the Louth Mail, running twelve minutes behind, left the Great North Road.

During the Napoleonic War there was an extensive prisoner of war camp near Norman's Cross. The Post Office offered a reward to guards if they shot escaping prisoners. Unfortunately a number of innocent local people were peppered with buckshot by over enthusiastic guards, and the reward scheme was withdrawn.

In eight and a half miles the Mail reached Wansford, where the famous Haycock Inn once stabled over 150 horses. After changing they crossed the bridge over the River Nene and trotted towards Stamford to pass first the grounds of Burghley House. It is one of the largest Elizabethan houses in the country built by William Cecil, later Lord Burghley, whose ancestors lived in Stamford. He was Secretary of State for the greater part of Queen Elizabeth's reign, and her regard for him was sufficient for her to travel from London to visit him during his last illness.

At a quarter past five in the morning the Mail arrived at the George at Stamford with its gallows sign stretching right across the

*Arriving at the
George, Stamford*

street. The George still retains two rooms, marked "London" and "York" which were waiting rooms for passengers, and at the rear its coaching yard. The fresh team would be harnessed and standing ready in St. Martin's Street as the coach came to a halt. In about one and a half minutes they were off again giving passengers no chance to explore this historic town.

At the time of the Domesday Book Stamford had a market, and by the 14th century it had become a prosperous wool town and an important religious centre, consisting of four monasteries and friaries, a number of hospitals, and fourteen churches. The fabric and prosperity of the town suffered considerably during the Wars of the Roses at the hands of the Lancastrians, and the monastic establishments which survived were dealt with by the Royal Commissioners around 1538. The Queen Anne and Georgian buildings in local grey stone have retained their elegance, and the town has still retained six of its original churches.

After the Edinburgh Mail pulled away from the George, it crossed the bridge over the River Welland, passed the Town Hall built in 1777, and the Church of St. Mary with its fine 13th century spire, to leave through Scotgate. The next stage of the journey was to Grantham.

Certain coachmen on this ground delighted in telling their box seat companion about Daniel Lambert. His tombstone records that he measured 3 feet and 1 inch around the leg, 9 feet and 4 inches around the body, and weighed 52 stone and 11 pounds. He died in 1809 aged thirty-nine years and was buried in St. Martin's churchyard.

The fresh team pulled hard on the long steady climb; at Stretton a change was made and the coachman, thinking of breakfast, kept his team moving well.

Up St. Peter's Hill and into the High Street the sweating horses cantered with the Mail. No real command was needed from the coachman, they knew exactly when to come back to a trot and stop at the George at Grantham, which Dickens said was "one of the best inns in all England". Three long blasts on the guard's horn announced their arrival. They had travelled $106\frac{1}{2}$ miles in eleven hours and twenty-six minutes. The coach disgorged its passengers, weary, half asleep, hungry and possibly not particularly good tempered. Breakfast included ham and eggs or boiled eggs, hot rolls and butter and best Bohea (a black tea). While the Edinburgh passengers were enjoying this, their coachman wished them well, with his hand extended, for the expected tips.

Before they had finished their meal, more horn calls outside, and in filed the Glasgow travellers. Also stiff, weary and disgruntled.

Waiters darted in all directions and everyone demanded to be served at once. Meanwhile the guard who had brought the mail from London was busy outside handing over to his successor. The mail bags had to be transferred to another coach and passengers' baggage stowed.

As can be seen from this portion of the Way-bill, the times were entered, the timepiece handed over and the Way-bill signed by the new guard.

DETAILS OF WAY-BILL

between Stamford and Newark

Contractor's Name	Miles and Furlongs	Time Allowed	
		H M	
T. Wincup {	8.5		
	6	1 32	Arrived at Stamford 5.14 a.m.
	8.0	0 50	,, ,, Stretton 6.04 ,,
H. Wincup {	5.1		Colsterworth
	8.1	1 22	Arrived at Grantham 7.26 a.m.
			By timepiece . . . . By clock
			. . . .
			Coach No. ⎰ Delivered the
			. . . . Gone ⎱ Time piece safe
			Forward ⎰ No. . . . .
			⎱ To . . . .
		40	Forty mins. allowed
Burbridge	6.0	0 36	Arrived at Foston 8.42 a.m.
Lawton	8.0	0 48	,, ,, Newark 9.30 ,,

The new guard called the passengers to the coach, the old one watched, and thanked them for their tips.

Further down the High Street stands the Angel and Royal. There is a record that in 1213 it belonged to the Knights Templar who entertained King John there. In the following century it was rebuilt. The front is all that is left of the old house but it includes the State Room where Richard III signed the death warrant of Henry Stafford, Duke of Buckingham.

In the early 18th century a certain Michael Solomon left a bequest of £2 annually charged against the rent of the Angel to pay for a sermon to be preached each year denouncing the sin of drunkenness. The 14th century Church of St. Wulfram's, whose 272 feet spire dominates the town, was the place for this exhortation.

The new coachman put the fresh team at Gonerby Hill, 350 feet high and with a view over miles of Fenland. In one direction the cathedral at Lincoln and in the other the Vale of Belvoir and its famous castle.

They were due to change at the Black Horse, Foston, at eighteen minutes before nine and then continue to Newark. Upon reaching the Post Office bags were exchanged, a fresh team harnessed, and they were away again, trotting past the ruins of a fine castle. In 1216

King John died at Newark and James I stayed on his journey south in 1603. Later, in 1642, Newark stood for the king, and four years later paid the price. The town was ordered to lay down its arms and the castle was destroyed.

The Mail crossed Newark bridge at thirty-five minutes past nine o'clock, moving fast over a level road, but one often liable to flooding. The up Mail in midwinter worked most of this stage in darkness. Coachmen then had to judge the height of flood by the light from the coach lamp as the horses waded into the water. The insiders could hear the swish of water against the coach and usually stood on the seats with heads bowed against the roof waiting for the moment it forced through the doors of the coach. It would soak the straw on the floor, and sometimes even rose to the level of the seats. It must have been a frightening experience, leaving the insiders cold and wet afterwards. The guard also watched anxiously. If the floods were too deep to proceed with the coach, he had to wade in, unhitch one of the leaders, remove the mails from the box, swim with the horse carrying the bags, and proceed to the next stage. In the event of such a mishap, the coachman and the passengers were left to fend for themselves. Occasionally for feats of outstanding devotion to duty the guard was awarded an "ex gratia" payment of half a guinea, and sometimes a guinea.

At Scarthing Moor they were safe from flooding. The road they took was by way of Tuxford, West Retford and Barnby Moor.

They passed the Blue Bell Inn, where there was a huge horse pond, which must have been very suitable for washing down a dirty post-chaise. After three miles they trotted quickly through Scrooby without a thought for William Brewster, the Reverend Mr. Clifton, William Bradford and others who assembled each Sunday at the Manor House instead of attending divine service. For this offence they were imprisoned, and upon their release left the country. They were the senior members of the Pilgrim Fathers.

The Edinburgh Mail stopped at the Crown at Bawtry. William Adams the proprietor was also the Postmaster there. The fine stretch of road between Bawtry and Doncaster had no equal on the Great North Road. It was wide enough for four coaches to drive abreast. So as post-chaise and stage cantered towards them, the Mail swept imperiously towards Doncaster.

They arrived at the New Angel with four tired, dusty and foam flecked horses, but they were on time – twelve minutes past one. Thomas Pye, the landlord of the New Angel, also drove the Edinburgh Mail between Doncaster and Stamford and was well respected for his great ability as a whip.

To Doncaster in 1814 came an unknown artist named J. F. Herring. He obtained employment at Wood's Coach Offices driving coaches, and in his spare time painted animals on inn signs. Seven

*Floods near
Newark*

years later he could afford to throw down the ribbons and concentrate on his very successful career.

About this same coach office is told a story which could well be true. After the Napoleonic Wars there was a period when it was fashionable to name coaches after the celebrities and their achievements. A Frenchman visiting Doncaster asked the clerk to book a seat on the best coach to London.

"That will be the Lord Nelson", said the booking clerk.

"Damn your Lord Nelson", replied the Frenchman.

He was offered the Wellington, and after that the Waterloo, which upset him still further. He made some derogatory remarks about coaches in general and took a post-chaise instead – at, of course, much greater expense.

Another coachman took the ribbons for the journey to York. They left via French Gate to drive the fifteen miles to Ferrybridge, with a change at the Robin Hood Inn.

The Angel at Ferrybridge was a great rambling series of buildings, plain and austere with a vast area given up to stabling. It had coach houses, a chaise house and sleeping quarters for post-boys and ostlers at the rear. The inn had a considerable posting business, apart from horsing the Mails and stagecoaches, and day and night post-chaise rattled over the stone pavement, through the dark archway to the yard beyond. Often they horsed over fifty pairs a day, apart from teams required for the coaches.

The Mails reached the Rose & Crown, Tadcaster, at four minutes to four in the afternoon and no time was lost here; letter bags exchanged and a fresh team harnessed in less than two minutes. The ten miles to York is a level road so they rushed through Street Houses, and Dring Houses, possibly scattering fowls, cats and dogs, as they made for the city.

Under Mickelgate Bar, over the Ouse Bridge swept the Mail watched by old men and boys, as it whipped round the sharp corner into Spurriergate, through the narrow confines of Coney Street to arrive at six minutes to five outside the York Tavern, which stood next to the Post Office in St. Helen's Square.

During the last few years, prior to being taken off the road in 1842, the Edinburgh Mail travelled by way of Selby.

9 The Edinburgh Mail

York to Edinburgh by way of Berwick

Still retaining its four ancient gates, the city walls, and within them its ancient streets and buildings, York has preserved much of its heritage from the past.

Apart from the origin of its name Jorvic, a reminder of Danish occupation, a considerable part of the first half of the 2,000 years of the city's history was obliterated when William the Conqueror repulsed the Danes in 1069. However, he brought peace which had not been experienced with any certainty during the previous 600 years.

This peace brought prosperity. The following three centuries saw the great Minster built, the city rebuilt and the title of Lord Mayor conferred by Richard II. Trade with the Low countries and beyond developed, resulting in the importance of the city's Trade Guilds, who in many cases established their own halls and chapel. The Merchant Adventurers of York built their hall near Fossgate. A further reminder of their activities, now revived, were the Medieval Mystery Plays, in which each Guild enacted a story from the Bible.

The Minster was not a monastic foundation. Around 627 AD the first wooden church existed, and the Normans replaced a stone building which they had destroyed. Not until 1225 was the work on the present Cathedral started, and more than 250 years elapsed before the entire building was completed.

The grandeur and elegance of this great church is everywhere, both externally and internally. Honey coloured stone bathed in light which penetrates the many beautiful windows. The vitality of the colours of medieval glass, the immense length and height of nave and choir, and the glory of the perfect 14th century Chapter House.

The city was spared much of the ravages which might have ensued during the Civil War, the citizens agreeing to surrender on reasonable terms. These were accepted by the Parliamentary General Fairfax, whose family came from Yorkshire.

The late 17th century saw the beginning of the impact of coaching on the city. An advertisement dated 12th April, 1706 gave notice of the commencement of a "Four day Stage Coach to London", referring to a York to Newcastle stage already in existence. By the 19th century coaching had become an important business. The principal inns were the George in Coney Street, a posting inn in 1700, the Black Swan, also in Coney Street, which began running stagecoaches in 1706, Etteridge's Hotel in Lendal which supplied horses only for post-chaise and the York Tavern,

Travelling North

St. Helen's Square, where the Mails stopped. Smaller coaching inns included the White Horse in Coppergate, the White Swan, Nessgate and many others. Due to the foresight of one man, George Hudson, as the coaching declined the city took advantage of the new form of transport, the railway.

Although the infamous Dick Turpin was tried at York Assizes in March, 1739, and hanged the following month, he was not convicted this time of robbing a coach. From May, 1737, when he shot his confederate, Matthew King at the Old Red Lion, Aldgate, there had been a price of £200 on his head. He went to ground until, in October, 1738, he surfaced using the name of Palmer. He was taken to York prison under this name on suspicion of horse stealing. Turpin wrote to his brother-in-law in Essex asking him to stand bail. The brother-in-law refused to accept the letter and pay the postage and therefore the local postmaster opened the letter. He knew Dick Turpin, he knew also about the £200 reward, so he hastened to York. On his evidence "Palmer" was tried as Dick Turpin. The myth of the gallant highwayman, and the romance surrounding his ride to York, are purely fictional.

Another coach was to "go forward" to Berwick therefore the mails and luggage had to be transferred. The new guard took over the timepiece, and Way-bill from his predecessor. This was the timesheet which covered the entire journey to Edinburgh and could therefore not be returned to London until this was accomplished. The authorities devised a "short bill" which was a duplicate of the Way-bill proper as far as York. After the guard had completed the relevant details it was despatched to London on the next up Mail, having the effect of confirming or otherwise that the first part of the journey had been completed with or without incident.

Short bills were used on all those mails taking over twenty-four hours to reach their destination.

At thirty-four minutes past five in the afternoon the Edinburgh Mail left the city passing the Mansion House completed in 1726 as the Lord Mayor's residence during his term of office. They passed under Bootham Bar, where armed guards were once stationed to conduct travellers through the Forest of Galtres to protect them from wolves.

The stage to Easingwold was an easy one by way of Clifton, Skelton and Shipton. A road of wide grass verges, which cut through the flat countryside interspersed with woods, copses, and windmills. Long Street, Easingwold, is a by-pass for the village itself, with its church and charming houses, clustered around the green hidden away to the east. The Mail drew up at the New Inn to change at six minutes before seven. This inn, which still stands in the wide street, maintained a number of post-boys and horses, as did all the inns on this road.

The change at the
Golden Fleece,
Thirsk

GOLDEN FLEECE

Many of these post-boys were great characters, and one remembered until the turn of the century was "wee Billy Barnes", employed at the New Inn all his working life. He is credited with having ridden the Stage to Thirsk and back six times in a day, a distance of 120 miles. Taken as a class these men were tough and wiry, for in pursuit of their business they had to undergo many hardships. Not infrequently on their return in bitter weather, they were so stiff with cold they had to be lifted out of the saddle.

Another gentle stage to Thirsk, where on the west side of the cobbled square stands the Golden Fleece which has changed little since the time the Edinburgh Mail stopped each evening. Indeed portraits of Mr. John Hill and his son, who kept this inn during the first half of the last century still hang on the staircase.

Nine miles to Northallerton. An uninteresting road with the Cleveland Hills rising in the distance on the east side.

On these hills was bred the Yorkshire Coach Horse. Strong, long-striding horses with enough stamina to maintain the rigours of the stage they worked. Cleveland Bays also were great favourites with the coachmen.

The team harnessed at Thirsk stopped outside the Golden Lion at Northallerton, a fine Georgian inn, with a splendid porch surmounted by a rather benevolent lion. Through the archway at the end of the building is the yard, where once they stabled 100 horses. Yet another inn which would be recognised by the coachmen working this ground, if they were alive today.

From the Golden Lion they continued on a wide road over Lovesome Hill, to pause at the Blacksmith's Arms at Great Smeaton to change the horses. This old inn, which was later converted into cottages, was kept by three generations of Tweedies. Mr. William Tweedie, who combined the business of innkeeper with that of postmaster, was once asked by a rather condescending traveller how long he had been at the Blacksmith Arms, to which he replied "why friend would you believe it I came to this house without a shirt to my back". He paused before adding "I was born here".

The Mail left the Blacksmith's Arms with only nine miles to cover to reach Darlington, passing through Dalton, over Croft Bridge which spans the River Tees, to pull up at the Kings Head at twenty-eight minutes past ten.

Defoe, in the mid-17th century, described this town rather unkindly as "a post town which has nothing remarkable in it but dirt, and a high bridge over little or no water".

The principal bankers in Darlington at this time were Backhouse & Co. (now part of Barclays Bank). Jonathan Backhouse, a respected citizen, was the senior partner in the firm. Early in the 19th century for reasons unknown a dispute arose between Lord Darlington and the Quaker bankers. His Lordship notified his tenants that their rents must be paid in Backhouse notes. He intended to "break the Bank" by suddenly presenting so large a number that they could not all be honoured in gold. Mr. Backhouse heard of the plot and immediately posted to London for additional bullion.

On his return when passing over Croft Bridge, one of the fore-wheels of the chaise broke. Knowing the urgency of his mission he refused to wait for the wheel to be replaced. The banker piled the bags of gold on one side of the back of the coach and drove into Darlington on three wheels! He was just in time, and Lord Darlington's agents expressed considerable surprise when the notes they presented were promptly honoured in gold. The banker gave them a message. "Now tell thy master if he will sell his favourite horse I will pay for that in the same metal."

The incident is confirmed by entries in the books of the Bank:

```
1819   6m   25th   To Bank and cash London £32,000
       7m   31st   Debited to Profit and Loss a/c
                    £2–3–0 for wheel demolished.
```

While the coach waited at the King's Head few might recall that the first railway was opened in 1825 between Stockton and Darlington. Eleven years later railways were being constructed between Liverpool and Birmingham and London and Birmingham.

At thirty-three minutes past ten the coaches trotted up the long rise of Harrowgate Hill to Coatham Mundeville. After passing through Aycliffe, they drove over an undulating road to Rushyford, where the inn was a Mail Receiving Office, which also provided a fresh team to haul the coach to Durham.

The River Wear was crossed at Sunderland Bridge. Again it was crossed as the Mail moved quickly over the Elvet Bridge and into the lower half of the city of Durham, to change at the Waterloo Inn.

Above them stood the proud Norman castle which never fell to Scottish invaders. It guards the massive building of the cathedral whose strength, like that of the castle, seems to stem from the hard rock on which it stands. To an outsider who saw this in the moonlight it was perhaps the memory of a lifetime.

The origin of Durham Cathedral is a party of monks from Lindisfarne, constantly threatened by the Danes, seeking a new resting place for the body of their saint. They chose this stone outcrop defended on three sides by the River Wear. Their choice was perfect and, in 998, they reburied the remains of St. Cuthbert in the "White Church". Almost 100 years later the foundation of the present building was laid by Bishop William of Calais. Only forty years had elapsed when most of the plan envisaged by this bishop had materialised and the bones of St. Cuthbert reinterred in a tomb behind the High Altar. The cathedral is the finest example of early Norman architecture in the country.

About 4,000 of the Scottish prisoners captured by Cromwell after the battle of Dunbar were shut up in Durham Cathedral. They were not only hungry but cold so they broke up and burnt the medieval woodwork in the cathedral in an endeavour to keep warm.

The Mail left Durham at thirty-five minutes past twelve o'clock, trotted down Silver Street, across the Framwell Gate Bridge, and turned north for Chester-le-Street where they stopped for the change. Then they headed for Gateshead and Newcastle.

On this road about three miles to the east lies the little village of Washington. It was the home of the Wessyngton family, the direct ancestors of George Washington, America's first president. Prior John of Wessyngton was appointed early in the 15th century to carry out a programme of extensive repairs to Durham Cathedral. The present house built in the 17th century is now a museum.

The approach to Newcastle through Gateshead was a steep descent to the Tyne bridge called Bottlebank. A new bridge completed in 1781 replaced an earlier one swept away by flood waters ten years previously. The coachman sprang the team as they crossed the bridge to meet the challenge of Sandhill on the other side. Up the Side and into Dean Street they trotted passing the church of St. Nicholas, now the cathedral, to stop at the Queen's Hotel.

It was the new castle built by Henry II from which the town took its name. During the Civil War the town was besieged by the Scots and suffered considerable damage. The beautiful parish church with its 15th century "crown spire" was saved by the mayor placing Scottish prisoners in the tower when the enemy threatened to set fire to the building. In the last years of the coaching era, as if anticipating railways and change, John Dobson and Richard Grainger planned and rebuilt part of the city in a uniform architectural style which is much admired today.

Still nearly 125 miles the Mail must travel to reach Edinburgh. After five minutes had elapsed they were off again north to Morpeth, Alnwick and the border. They climbed past Town Moor where the city fairs are held, and travelled over an exposed road where nothing prevented a bleak northerly wind cutting through those on the top of the coach. Insiders were more fortunate, but they had to endure the constant stamping of outsiders' feet endeavouring to keep warm. On nights such as these the change at the Sun at Stannington called for a quick brandy and hot water. There was no time for a second as they were due at Morpeth at twenty-two minutes past three.

Across Telford's new bridge (built 1831) and up the main street of the town to the Queen's Head. The road climbs out of the town to Warreners' House, a toll gate, and runs north to Earsdon Moor through country dotted with Peel towers, a reminder of the constant strife on the border. Eventually they descended to Felton Bridge over the River Coquet and into the village where the Northumberland Arms also acted as a Mail office.

From here in fifty minutes they reached Alnwick, a grey town set in beautiful countryside. For centuries the Percy's from their castle fortress ruled much of the north of England and held it against the Scots despite frequent border feuds.

They left the White Swan, Alnwick, at twenty past five, passed under the Hotspur Tower, the only surviving gateway of the town walls and drove along a road which descends to the bridge of the River Aln. Looking back, there is a view of the grey and formidable castle. From here a hard climb to the summit of Hefferlaw Bank. Then towards Belford with continuous views of the Northumberland coast, Beadnell Bay, Seahouses, Bamburgh, and beyond the distant Farne Islands.

The rocks around these islands have claimed many ships, although one is remembered because of the outstanding courage of a young woman. In September, 1838 the *Forfarshire* bound for Dundee struck the Big Harcar rocks and broke in two. Grace Darling's father was the keeper of the Longstone light, and between them they launched their tiny boat in mountainous seas. Nine survivors were found on the rocks, which meant two trips back to the lighthouse with Grace helping to row the boat. When news of this deed spread Grace Darling became a national heroine. Only four years later she died from tuberculosis and was buried in Bamburgh churchyard.

Entering Belford at thirteen minutes to seven the Mails would have seen, standing on a corner with the church behind, the Blue Bell, with its Georgian style windows and porch, mellow brick and creeper. It is a most attractive building and was granted a licence in 1812 due to the lack of posting inns on this part of the road. With a fresh team already waiting the Mail stayed less than two minutes. This did not allow enough time to see the Minstrel's Gallery which overlooks a well proportioned Banqueting Hall within the inn.

The road continues to run almost parallel to the coast, looking down on the island of Lindisfarne.

Somewhere near Fenwick in 1685 occurred a rather unusual "hold-up". Grizel Cochrane, disguised as a man and mounted on horseback, waylaid a Special Messenger. At pistol point she robbed him of the warrant he was carrying for the execution of her father, Sir John Cochrane, for his part in a rebellion against James II. By this act she obtained a fortnight's grace during which time Sir John's friends were able to secure his pardon.

Berwick was reached by way of a stone bridge of fifteen arches built in the early 17th century across the River Tweed. From this vantage point the estuary widens out towards the sea, and the town is still surrounded by walls which enclose its grey stone buildings with their red tiled roofs, and its cobbled streets. The walls serve as a reminder of the times when Berwick was constantly fought over, changing hands more than twelve times before finally, in 1482, it became English territory.

The Mail quickly made its way through Bridge Street and turned up Hide Hill. Here at the King's Arms breakfast was served at seventeen minutes past eight. Waiting to carry the mail to Edinburgh was the Scottish coach, which differed only from its English counterpart by allowing four outsiders instead of three. The extra seat could be useful in the transfer of prisoners usually undertaken by the Mails on the basis of one warder to two prisoners. Letters to and from Scotland were charged an additional ½d. to offset the cost of tolls, which in the case of the journey from here to Edinburgh amounted to £1.

At three minutes to nine the Mail set off for the Scottish capital with a fresh team, coach, coachman and guard. A lawyer who travelled the road regularly during the last years of the coaches related how once he had to endure rainwater trickling down his neck from a crack in the roof. At Berwick he mentioned this to the coachman and received the terse reply:

"Ay, mony a one 'as complained o' that 'ole."

The Edinburgh Mail approached the Lamberton Bar. There is a notice on this former tollhouse to the effect that the Keepers of the gate once performed marriage ceremonies similar to those in existence at Gretna Green until 1856. The gate was open as the Scottish Post Office settled tolls directly with the turnpike authorities. On a fine summer morning how pleasant it must have been to drive this coast road, but in winter there were times when every mile seemed like two, as the horses, heads bowed, trotted into a relentless northerly wind.

Quite suddenly the road turns inland and descends to the bridge over the River Eye and into Ayton. A further change was made at Houndwood after which they drove through a beautiful wooded valley in the Lammermuir hills, past Grant's House to enter Cockburnspath. They quickly changed at the King's Arms and left for the town of Dunbar.

Carlyle wrote:

> The small town of Dunbar stands high and windy, looking down over its herring boats, over its grim old castle, now much honeycombed on one of those projecting rock-promontories with which that shore of the Firth of Forth is niched and vandyked as far as the eye can reach. A beautiful sea: good land too, now that the plougher understands his trade: a grim niched barrier of whinstone sheltering it from the chafings and tumblings of the big blue German Ocean.

They hurried up the wide main street of this town between houses built of dark red stone, changed at the St. Andrew's Inn, and hurried on again over the cobbles leaving behind the Old Town House built in 1620.

The coach covered the eleven miles to Haddington in just over an hour to reach the Bell & George at a quarter to one. They only stopped to change, so hungry passengers must wait until Edinburgh. They passed the Mercat Cross surmounted by the figure of a goat and the Town House designed by William Adam.

Approaching Musselburgh there is a fine view of the Firth of Forth stretching to the distant coast of Fife. Musselburgh was excommunicated for two centuries because about 1591 it dared to build its Tolbooth from the stones of the Chapel of our Lady of Loretto. At the Boar's Head in the town the last change was made. They would be in Edinburgh within the hour.

They drove along the London road, turned to descend Abbey Hill making for Canongate.

Dominating the city the castle rock with its fortress, and to the east, King Arthur's seat, a miniature mountain beneath which lies the Palace of Holyrood. Between these two hills, the old town with its closes and wynds astride the streets of Lawnmarket, High Street, and Canongate. The buildings are vivid reminders of the wealth of history attached to Edinburgh, which in the 18th century expanded westward from Carlton Hill according to the ideas of Provost Drummond. A young architect named James Craig was the author of the successful plans which included building Princes Street and George Street. His work was further enhanced by men such as Robert Adam, who created Charlotte Square. Thus old and new have fused together into a most attractive city.

The oldest building in Edinburgh is a stone shrine on the castle rock known as St. Margaret's Chapel. This lady, Queen of King Malcolm of Scotland, and sister of Edgar Atheling, on her death bequeathed to her son, David I, a gold casket said to contain a piece of the cross. For safekeeping he gave it to the Augustine monks of the abbey he founded near the city, which became known as the Holy Rood. Regrettably two centuries later the English stole the relic and placed it in Durham Cathedral where, during the Reformation, it was lost.

For three generations the Scottish kings used the guest house of the abbey as their residence, until in 1503 James IV commenced the building of a palace. Forty years later, Henry VIII, furious with the decision of their Parliament to annul the marriage treaty he had made between his son Edward and Mary, Queen of Scots, sent Lord Protector Somerset to teach them a lesson, which resulted in the firing of both the abbey and the palace. Obviously some of the damage must have been made good for later on James VI lived at Holyrood until he acceded to the English throne.

Finally the palace was almost totally destroyed by fire when Cromwell's troops were quartered there after the Battle of Dunbar in 1650. Fire could not destroy the memories of murder and intrigue surrounding Mary, Queen of Scots' stay in Edinburgh Castle.

After the Restoration, Charles II ordered the complete reconstruction of his Scottish palace, which remains to this day, while the abbey stands nearby in ruins.

It was at the White Horse close in Canongate where in these times they stabled around 100 horses, that the Edinburgh Mail arrived at twenty-three minutes past two in the afternoon, a journey of $399\frac{3}{4}$ miles in forty-two hours twenty-three minutes.

At four o'clock another coach left the city for those passengers and mails bound for Aberdeen, to arrive at twenty-seven minutes past six o'clock the following morning.

10 The Norwich Mail

Travelling by way of Colchester and Ipswich

Exeter, served by three Mails, was the most favoured city in the country but travellers to Norwich had the good fortune of a choice of two. The fastest by way of Chelmsford, Colchester and Ipswich arrived at thirty-eight minutes past seven in the morning, while the other travelling via Newmarket and Bury St. Edmunds reached the city at five minutes past nine.

At St. Martin's le Grand passengers arranged for their luggage to be handed over to the guard and it was placed in the front boot of the coach. Not surprisingly there were limits on the amount each passenger was allowed. *Instructions to Guards* in 1829 stated:

> No more than 3 articles, Portmanteau, or Carpet Bags, are on any pretence to be allowed, whether they be large or small. Portmanteau is not to exceed 2 feet 4 inches in length, and 1 foot 6 inches in height. By Portmanteau is meant any articles made of or covered in Leather or Hair, and Boxes of other Materials, Bundles, Baskets etc. are to be rejected. No luggage to be allowed on the roof until the front boot is full, and only then if the space is not required for additional mail bags.

With the increase in the volume of post being carried by the mid-1830s, letter bags were often carried on the roof of the coach, and this is confirmed by Cooper Henderson's paintings at this time.

Yarmouth, and the two Norwich Mails, left together, and moved through the narrow streets of Cheapside, Leadenhall Street to Aldgate High Street where a number of inns were clustered serving the stagecoaches, post-chaise, and waggons using this road. The inns included the Three Nuns, Saracen's Head, Blue Boar, and the renowned Bull owned by Mrs. Nelson and later her son John.

The High Street broadened out into Whitechapel Road, and in the fine thoroughfare was held the twice-weekly Hay and Straw market. The entire street was packed with great farm waggons which had been drawn into town by chestnut coloured heavy horses from distant parts of Essex and Suffolk. Ale flowed freely at the inns, there was constant shouting, bargaining, and merriment, and the smell of hay and horses.

At the corner of Leman Street and Whitechapel Road stood the Old Red Lion. To this old galleried inn Dick Turpin was traced after stealing a valuable horse near Epping. The Bow Street runners found him in the company of his confederates Tom and Matthew King, and in the struggle which followed to resist arrest Turpin

*The Norwich and
Yarmouth Mails in
Aldgate High Street*

shot Matthew King. Whether it was by design or an accident is uncertain. However, King later died of his wounds, cursing Turpin who had escaped.

The coaches passed Whitechapel Church, the point from which the roads to East Anglia were measured, and soon approached the Mile End turnpike. Rowlandson's picture of 1813 portrays a very wide road, two sets of gates, with a keeper's lodge on each side, while in the centre was a tall standard of three huge gas lights. Only two Mails passed through the gate, as the Newmarket Mail had already turned north heading for Hackney.

The broad highway continued to Stratford le Bow, where the parish church stands in the middle of the road. In the time of Henry I a stone causeway was built over the marsh, and a stone arched bridge constructed over the River Lea. The semi-circular arch was unusual in these times and may be the origin of the name Bow.

The Mails trotted fast through the village of Ilford and drove together over a road which crossed Chadwell Heath, a lonely landscape of stunted thorn trees and gorse. In the hamlet of Chadwell Heath itself stood the Whalebone House which appeared under the name of "Ye Whalebone" on Ogilby's map of 1698. Two large bones affixed on either side of the gateway were supposed to have been taken from the body of a whale stranded in the Thames in 1658. Quite possibly coachmen enjoyed telling this story as they made their way along the road, and after 1829 could include the details of the brutal murder of the gatekeeper at Chadwell Heath while he was robbed of the tolls.

Both the Yarmouth and Norwich Mails arrived at the White Hart at Romford at twelve minutes past nine. In the 1830s Romford was a pleasant market town of around 4,000 inhabitants, renowned for the brewing of good ale, and the making of excellent breeches. There was a saying in the county: "Get'e to Romford and get yer backside new bottomed."

On Wednesdays, the weekly market day, the square was full of cattle, sheep, pigs, horses, carts, gigs, and waggons. There were farmers and country folk gossiping, and stallholders chatting with their customers. Stagecoach or chaise were forced to edge their excited horses slowly through this noisy throng. At night the square was empty.

After leaving Romford the Mails passed the Unicorn in Hare Street, through the tollgate at Puttles Bridge (now Putwell). At Brentwood letter bags were dropped at the post office, but they did not stop at the fine White Hart Inn which retains within its yard the old timber galleries dating from the 15th century.

It was always dark as they crossed Shenfield Common. A lonely location which may have caused the guards to worry about the possibility of a breakdown and to hope at least this time they would be fortunate. Upon enlistment guards were given a fortnight's training at Vidler's Coachyard at Millbank, to enable them to deal with minor problems, and the coach carried spares and tools. By now, tried and proved over many years the construction of the vehicle was robust enough to run without many breakdowns, especially as it was checked at the end of each journey. Poor harness was more of a problem as contractors were loath to spend too much of their profits in this direction, especially on stages run in darkness. Traces, subject to chafing and pulling, could break without warning. If they did, the guard must repair them quickly. The incident, and length of delay, would be entered on the timesheet to enable those at Post Office headquarters to know which contractor was at fault. There were cases where after repeated warnings the Post Office sent the culprit a new set of harness, the cost of which was charged against his dues!

The two Mails trotted through Mountnessing Street, a village today but then a cluster of cottages, a windmill, and a milestone which read "Ingatestone 2".

Twelve minutes later they had covered the two miles to Ingatestone, where the red brick church tower looks down on the narrow street. They stopped at the Spread Eagle for a change of horse at eighteen minutes past ten.

At Margareting Street mail bags were exchanged without a stop at the Post Office. The postmaster had to be waiting at the roadside, pass up to the guard any mail in a bag hung at the end of a long pole, and pick up the one literally dropped alongside him.

The entrance to Chelmsford was over an attractive stone-arched bridge built in 1787. Straight ahead the High Street at the end of which stands the church of St. Mary, St. Peter and St. Cedd, now the cathedral. Apart from the Saracen's Head, most of Chelmsford's old coaching inns have been pulled down.

Anthony Trollope, who was travelling inspector in the employ of the Post Office, was staying at the Saracen's Head at the time his Barchester tales were being issued in weekly instalments. A party were discussing Mrs. Proudie, the bishop's wife, over coffee and one was heard to say "Confound the woman! I for one wish she were dead!" Trollope introduced himself, thanked the assembled company for the idea and promised that she would die in the next instalment. She did!

After crossing the bridge the Mails turned right by the conduit, skirted the town, and drove towards Springfield and the Black Boy. For 400 years an inn of this name had existed here before being demolished in 1857. At the Black Boy a fresh team was harnessed.

In 1883 the Post Office discovered it was paying far too much of its gross receipts in the parcel business to the railways for the carriage between towns and decided to run its own parcel service, cutting them out. The pilot scheme ran between London and Ipswich each night, which as far as Colchester was conveyed by a four-horsed Mail, and then to Ipswich by van. So after a break of nearly forty years the Mails were travelling again through the night on this road. Their speed of about seven miles per hour was slow enough to cause some astonishment amongst the older generation, who remembered the "better days".

It was a quarter to twelve when the Norwich and Yarmouth Mails trotted down the long street of Witham flanked by Georgian and Queen Anne buildings to pull up at the White Hart where they stopped twenty minutes for refreshment.

The Blue Pots at Witham was the dining place of Mrs. Nelson's famous stage "The Ipswich Blues" taking just over six hours to cover the seventy miles between Ipswich and her inn, the Bull at Aldgate. The performance of this prestige coach was only achieved by changes every six miles and placing extra horses ready at the foot of any stiff hills. For such a superb service there is no record of the fare charged!

At five minutes past midnight the two Mails left the White Hart to cover the fourteen miles to Colchester. In the long street of Kelvedon, bags were dropped at the Post Office and they trotted on through level countryside towards Mark's Tey. A land without stone, where timber, brick and flint were the materials used in the building of cottages. There were large rich pastures used for rearing strong cattle and small fields devoted to the growing of teasel.

After Mark's Tey there is an easy descent into the Colne Valley. From here the coaches drove through Crouch Street, negotiated the sharp turn into Head Street before they reached the broad thoroughfare of the High Street in which the principal inns of the town of Colchester were situated.

The half-timbered Red Lion has a long history for beneath the present 16th century building are vaults of earlier centuries. It is mentioned in records of 1515, and in 1604 when it was licensed as the "Wyn taverne" it was referred to as "an ancient inn".

The building is full of magnificent oak beams, many of which are carved, and the finest carving of all is the George and the Dragon on the spandrels of the early 16th century entrance archway.

Early stagecoaches were advertised as using the Red Lion. *The Ipswich Journal* in February, 1756 advertised:

> James Unwin, late coachman to Mr. Hills in Colchester, begs to inform the Publick that on Thursday, 9th March, he sets out from the Red Lyon Inn at Colchester, with a STAGE CART and able horses . . . to the Bell Inn Leadenhall Street.

In the *Journal* five years later it was announced that the Farewell Post Chaise would travel between the Red Lyon, Colchester, and the Green Dragon, Whitechapel, in eight hours at a cost of 6d. per mile. The Red Lion continued to remain an important posting inn, but the Mails used the Three Cups on the opposite side of the street.

In the early 19th century the Cups was a modern inn and the Red Lion old fashioned. In 1807 the Cups advertised in the local newspaper that it had "The Elegant Large New Room for Assemblies, and Balls", and many distinguished guests came to enjoy its hospitality, including Louis XVIII of France, and in 1817 George IV. Four years later his unhappy wife, Caroline, died having expressed a wish to be buried in Brunswick. The cortege left London for Harwich amidst wild scenes which *The Times* for 14th August, 1821 described as "Indecent haste . . . the procession hurried through the city at a trot." After that progress must have been slow for late in the afternoon of the following day the escort halted outside the Cups and left the coffin unattended in the street while they took refreshment inside.

At this time Colchester still possessed the Ancient Moot Hall (rebuilt later as the present Town Hall) where for centuries past the mayor and justices dealt with offences of all kinds from petty thieving to heresy.

The Mails left quickly to drive the next stage giving passengers no chance to obtain even a glimpse of the enormous Keep of the Norman Castle. Nor did they have even a taste of the town's renowned oysters, though guards on the up Mails doubtless carried oysters to London for some remuneration.

Before reaching Stratford St. Mary the road descends quite sharply to a bridge over the River Stour. The river meanders picturesquely between the grey green willows and red brown alders which line its banks. Flowing through a land of green meadows and fine cornfields, a land of noble oaks and elm, slowly the river makes its way in loops and bends past Dedham church and the Mill at Flatford to glide eventually into a broad tidal estuary. This is Constable country.

Into Suffolk and on towards Ipswich they travelled. It was on this road that in 1822 the Ipswich Mail was involved in a daring robbery when bank notes to the value of £31,000 were stolen. The Post Office were quick to offer a reward of £200, and such was the seriousness of the crime the bankers concerned offered £1,000 for information leading to an arrest. About £3,000 of the notes had been cashed before the banks involved gave notice that they had changed the colour of the printing ink they used thereby rendering the notes unusable. They endeavoured through a third party to negotiate for the recovery of the remainder. The thieves had the impudence to ask for £6,000, but the bankers refused and waited. Eventually about £28,000 of useless notes were recovered but the culprits were never traced.

*Floundering in
drifts on the
Norwich Road*

As the Norwich and Yarmouth Mails neared Ipswich they descended into the broad valley of the Orwell described by Cobbett on his ride:

> There were windmills on the hillocks so numerous that while standing in one place I counted no fewer than seventeen, all painted or washed white, with black sails.

They trotted up Corn Hill, turned into Tavern Street making a considerable noise to arrive at the Mail Office and Great White Horse at fourteen minutes past three in the morning. The post office stood opposite on the corner of Brook Street. In the course of five minutes the letter bags were exchanged and a fresh team harnessed. There was an inn here in 1518, which some three hundred years later was rebuilt. Practically everyone of importance travelling this road stayed at the Great White Horse including royalty, Lord Nelson and not surprisingly Mr. Pickwick.

The coaches left the town in different directions, Yarmouth by way of Carr Street and Norwich along Northgate. Neither of them passed the 15th century Ancient House in the Butter Market or Silent Street where probably around 1471 Cardinal Wolsey was born.

Ipswich suffered badly in the great blizzard of 1836 as this extract from the *Suffolk Chronicle* confirms:

> The extraordinary and almost unprecedented snow storm which commenced on Friday night, and has continued with little interruption up to the present time, has completely put a stop to the transaction of all business in this part of the country. The regularity of the mails, coaches etc. has been completely disorganised, and in some instances no communication whatever with several important towns in the neighbourhood of Ipswich has taken place since the commencement of the fall . . . some cases the ground is left completely bare . . . others drifts varying in depth from 4 to 20 feet.
>
> . . . . On Thursday, the accumulated posts for Norwich were dispatched under the care of James Cooper, also an Ipswich letter-carrier, by post-chaise. It was so found, however, that the roads were impassable by any vehicle beyond Stonham. He was therefore under the necessity of procuring a horse, and he proceeded onwards with his load which filled two sacks towards his destination. He arrived safely, and returned to Ipswich yesterday.
>
> His description of the journey justifies the general report that the roads in the direction of Norwich are obstructed to as great an extent as any others in the neighbourhood.

For occasions such as this the guard carried the *Snow Book* to be completed as well as the Way-bill!

GENERAL POST OFFICE

DECEMBER 1830

SNOW BOOK

In this book the Guard will carefully fill up the columns, either when Leaders are used for the Mails or Chaises, or Saddle Horses are taken in this Winter on account of Snow.

The duty of the Guard is always to keep the Mail Coach going in its regular manner, unless he sees a necessity of Assistance to prevent great loss of time. It will be the particular duty of the Guard to make a good arrival in London. When the time can be tolerably kept with the Leaders, it is the proper mode to take them, and never to have a chaise, unless the Coach, with its whole Load, cannot travel at all.

The Guard is still to mark on the Time Bills in the usual manner when Horses are had, and is to keep this Book the better to enable Mr. Johnson to cheque the Bills when received. A copy of the Book, twice a week, is to be sent to Mr. Johnson.

Date	From what Place	To what Place	No of Miles	By whom Supplied and whether Leaders or otherwise	Reason	By Guards order or not	For Guards Signature and any Remarks

(Post Office Records)

The fresh team harnessed at Ipswich pulled the coach easily up the long gentle climb to Whitton before descending to Claydon where any letter bags were exchanged at the Crown Inn.

The Norwich road then leaves the valley of the River Gipping heading north for Stonham. In midsummer dawn was breaking when they arrived at the "Pye" for a change of horse. From its gallows sign hung a large picture of a very saucy magpie, and outsiders new to the road often ducked as the coach passed underneath, although there was at least six inches to spare. The gallows are still there today but the present sign incorporates a magpie in a wrought iron "cage" above the beam.

In the early hours of each morning the Norwich Mail hurried over the next stage. It had dropped bags at the inns at Claydon and Stonham, both acting as post offices serving a considerable area, but how the inhabitants in remote hamlets and farms received their mail is best explained in a Treasury minute of 1841:

> In some places a messenger is employed to carry letters to and from the nearest Post Office (a distance occasionally of 10–15 miles) who is remunerated either by a subscription raised amongst the Inhabitants or more frequently by a fee charged on each letter. In other places a pauper performs the service, and thus the extra expense is reduced if not altogether avoided.
>
> . . . . In some cases it is stated that the Mail Guard, or other person employed in conveying the Mail through the village leaves the letters at an appointed place and obtains a fee generally a penny for each. But in numerous instances nothing like a systematic arrangement exists. One or two families perhaps have their own bags conveyed backwards and forwards at considerable expense, and others depend on the chance opportunities of calling at the Post Office (generally on Market days) or send whenever they hear by accident that a letter to their address is exposed in the Office window.

Those living in rural areas certainly fare better today.

At nine minutes past five the Mail arrived at the White Horse at Stoke, having covered eighty-six miles in just over nine hours. Quite often the horses supplied by the contractors on this road were Suffolk Punch, which although considered today as a breed of heavy horse, has excellent trotting qualities which suited the contractors' purpose well.

From Stoke a short stage of six miles through Yaxley and on towards the county border.

In the harvest season lines of sunburnt reapers had already started work, cutting steadily through the standing golden corn with their sickles while their womenfolk gathered it into stocks. They stopped for "Levenses" (mid-day meal) and again for

"Bever" (mid-afternoon) but continued work until dusk. At other times in the same fields green with young corn, there were just a few boys scaring off the birds with their rattles.

At forty-six minutes past five in the morning they arrived at the White Hart at Scole. It was built for James Peck, a merchant from Norwich, as an inn around 1655, at a time when there was little traffic on this road. Its fame lay in the fantastic gallows sign with twenty-five carved classical figures, and reputed to have cost over £1,000. At the beginning of the 19th century, although trade had much improved, it was taken down as the cost of repair was considered too great, and the ornate sign perished. So did the celebrated round bed supposed to have been capable of sleeping twenty couples! Both were used for firewood. Having discarded Peck's follies this splendid building remains today.

Straight as the flight of an arrow the road heads for Long Stratton where in a street of timber-framed houses stood the Swan, at which the last change was made before reaching Norwich.

The Mail approached Norwich from the south making for the gap in the city walls where once stood St. Stephen's Gate through which Elizabeth I entered the city on her visit in 1578.

The most spectacular approach to Norwich is from the north over Mousehold Heath, for from here can be seen the towers of the many medieval churches dominated by the lofty spire of the cathedral. John Crome, one of the founders of the Norwich School of Painters, frequently visited Mousehold to enjoy this view.

At the time of the Domesday Survey Norwich was one of the largest centres of population in the country, possessing also its own mint, over thirty churches but no cathedral.

The founder of the cathedral was Herbert de Losinga, who was appointed Bishop of Thetford in 1091. One does not know whether the story is true that he was guilty of simony in purchasing his preferment and the cathedral was built at his expense as a penance. It is certain, however, that he laid the foundation stone in 1096, and as a result of his encouragement and generosity a considerable part of the building was completed when he died in 1119. His successor finished the task in 1145. Stone from Caen, Normandy, was used on the exterior, and a canal was specially cut between the River Wensum and the site of the cathedral to transport the stone. It was three centuries later when above the superb Norman central tower the present spire was built. Rising to 305 feet it is almost as high as any hill in Norfolk.

Pestilence and civil strife seemed to haunt the city during the Middle Ages but Norwich survived. Towards the end of the 16th century immigrants from the Low Countries started to swell the population which had suffered the loss of one third of the citizens in yet another outbreak of plague. Gradually the important textile industry revived.

118

There exists an interesting description by Daniel Defoe made early in the 18th century:

> If a stranger was only to ride through or view the City of Norwich for a day he would have reason to think here was a town without inhabitants . . . . but on the contrary if he were to view the city either on a Sabbeth Day or on a public occasion he would wonder where all the people could dwell the multitude is so great; but the case is this. The inhabitants being all busy at their manufactures dwell in their garretts at their looms . . . . as almost all the works they are employed in being done within doors.

At this time the population of the city was around 25,000.

The latter years of this century saw the establishment of Gurney's Bank, the Norwich Union Insurance company and fresh industries resulting in a demand for better communications. The coaching business thrived with at least ten coaches running daily to London, but in the week before Christmas it was almost impossible to book a seat because the contractors found it more profitable to carry turkeys than passengers.

The Norwich Mail hurried up St. Stephen's Street making its way to the market place. Here on the south side is the beautiful church of St. Peter Mancroft, while on the east was the Angel Hotel. The time of arrival, thirty-eight minutes past seven, was less than twelve hours after leaving London, and the passengers had travelled 111 miles.

In 1845 the East Counties Railway was completed between London and Norwich.

11 The Dover Mail

*Travelling by way
of Rochester and
Canterbury*

Journeys by coach were always entered upon with a certain
amount of deliberation. There were decisions to be made: should it
be a day coach or a Mail. There was, as always, the question of cost;
inside was expensive, but because of the keen competition
between operators stage fares varied considerably. To be sure of
travelling on a particular coach it was necessary to book one's seat
usually a day or two before.

The Booking Office for the Dover Mail was at Mr. Horne's
establishment, the Golden Cross, at Charing Cross, described by
Dickens in *Sketches by Boz*:

> Porters, like so many Atlases, kept rushing in and out, with large
> packages on their shoulders; and while you are waiting to make
> the necessary enquiries you wonder what on earth the
> booking-office clerks can have been before they were booking-
> office clerks: one of them, with his pen behind his ear, and his
> hands behind him, is standing in front of the fire like a full-
> length portrait of Napoleon, the other with his hat half off his
> head, enters the passengers' names in the books with a coolness
> which is inexpressibly provoking; and the villain whistles –
> actually whistles – while a man asks him what the fare is outside
> all the way to . . . . and in frosty weather too! They are clearly an
> isolated race, evidently possessing no sympathies or feelings in
> common with the rest of mankind.

Booking-office clerks had to be efficient. If they over booked the
coach (as the proprietor had to carry every passenger booked) it
could mean the hire of a post-chaise to rectify the error, and this
cost would be deducted from their wages.

On the evening in question it would be necessary to arrive at the
yard of this inn well before half-past seven. Usually a two-horsed
vehicle, which doubtless had seen better days, would convey
passengers and luggage to St. Martin's-le-Grand for transfer to the
Dover Mail.

Prompt at eight o'clock they left, and the Dover Mail proceeded
down Cheapside and Poultry, passing the Mansion House before
turning into the new King William Street to approach London
Bridge (rebuilt 1831). Previously all traffic went through Lombard
Street into Gracechurch Street and down the steep descent of Fish
Hill. The Dover road was measured from the Southwick side of
London Bridge (half a mile from St. Martin's-le-Grand).

They trotted into Borough High Street, on the west side of which

120

The Golden Cross,
Charing Cross,
London

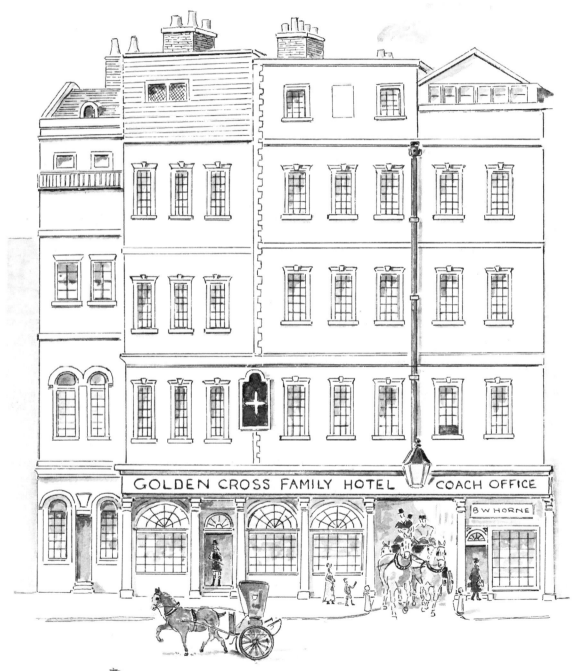

stands Southwick Cathedral. The fabric of St. Saviour's Church, as it was known at this time, was in a very poor condition but some restoration had already commenced. Shakespeare knew this church well for the site of the Globe Theatre is not far away.

In this High Street there were over twenty inns of considerable size standing back from the roadway with large wooden gates for protection. They were built in tiers of timbered galleries on three sides, overlooking their cobbled yards. One of these was the ancient Tabard, later called the Talbot, another the George, part of which remains today. The approaches to the city through Southwick were narrow, uncobbled streets, which were gradually improved in the course of time. Down the Old Kent Road they drove. A map of 1830 shows this district as a rural setting, just a few houses, most of which were drovers' inns.

In half an hour after leaving the General Post Office, the Dover Mail passed through New Cross. Only about fifty years previously Pitt and Dundas, overtaken by bad weather when travelling by post-chaise, were forced to spend the night at an inn here called the Golden Cross. If the details of their overnight stay are to be believed they drank seven bottles of port before retiring! It is certain that the conditions of these roads must have been appalling when two Cabinet Ministers thought it more prudent to stay at a drover's inn rather than continue the four miles to London.

Next through the dreary streets of Deptford, once a deep ford to be crossed by those using this road. A number of the ships which fought against the Spanish Armada were constructed in this dockyard, created by Henry VIII in 1513, and to the port came Drake's *Golden Hind* after circumnavigating the world.

After leaving Deptford the road ascends quite steeply to Blackheath, London's most historic common. Blackheath was the rallying point of those who, led by Wat the Tiler of Dartford in 1381, resented the Poll Tax and, almost seventy years later, Jack Cade assembled his rebellious followers on this heath. Here the Lord Mayor and Aldermen of the City of London with great ceremonial welcomed the return of King Henry V, after Agincourt. Another king, Charles II, returned under different circumstances to inspect the troops paraded on Blackheath, which included many veterans from the Battle of Worcester. There was a moment of suspense before first the crowds, then the troops, joined in a long ovation and escorted their new king to London. The problems surrounding the Restoration were overcome.

The coachman urged his team up the long climb of Shooters Hill, associated with robberies and highwaymen in fact as well as fiction. Byron also mentions Shooters Hill in his romantic poem *Don Juan*, as does Dickens in his *The Tale of Two Cities*. In the 1830s none dared to waylay the Royal Mail for the guard would not hesitate to use his firearms.

A minute after nine o'clock a fresh team was harnessed at the Bull, established as a sub-office in 1835, and they picked up the bye-bags. These contained letters for all the towns on the Dover Road and even some adjacent to it. From here they travelled the way which followed the line of the older Watling Street through Crayford to Dartford.

Older coachmen remembered many an exciting incident while entering or leaving Dartford. They skidded down West Hill and even with a fresh team in the days when passengers walked uphill, it was a very hard pull up the East Hill. Although improvements gradually were made to reduce the gradient of the approaches to this town, it was always an exhilarating experience to arrive safely at the Bull. This fine old galleried inn did not deign to display its sign as others did on the front of the building but fixed a metal silhouette of a large black bull on the chimney pots, high up for all to see.

In Dartford Church is the tomb of Sir John Spielman, who introduced the art of papermaking to this country and to this town in particular in the late 17th century.

There was a time when many travellers to Dover preferred to sail from London to Gravesend thence to continue their journey by road via Rochester and Canterbury. Whether James II in December, 1688 had any choice is not known but he disembarked at Gravesend, under escort, and the next day continued his journey to Dover.

After leaving the town it was a twisting and undulating road which took travellers through Chalk, where Charles Dickens spent his honeymoon, to Gad's Hill, which was his home from 1856 until his death.

The Mail hurried through the turnpike gate at Strood. From here, had it been daytime, the passengers would have had a marvellous view. Before one lay the broad valley of the Medway with numerous windmills placed on any elevated ground and red-sailed barges moving slowly on the river. Beyond this the city itself with the great keep of its ruined Norman castle, solid and challenging, and behind the ancient cathedral surrounded by the roofs of houses, shops and inns.

At twenty-six minutes to twelve the Dover Mail crossed the bridge on which Mr. Pickwick meditated "awaiting breakfast" when he and his party were staying at the Bull nearby. The coach then passed the red-bricked Guildhall opposite the Bull and drove up the High Street to the George near the Corn Exchange.

The creator of Mr. Pickwick describes the Exchange:

.... furnished with a queer clock that projects over the pavement out of a grave red-bricked building, as if time carried on a business, and hung out a sign.

The Dover Mail

The Mail stayed twenty-five minutes for refreshment. Time enough on a moonlight night to explore the High Street and obtain a glimpse of the cathedral. The present building stands on the site of a church founded by Bishop Justus in about 605 AD making it the second oldest See in the country. A considerable part of the strong Norman building commenced by Gundulph in 1080 survived a serious fire in 1179 and has been blended into later styles of architecture. Considerable funds were needed for rebuilding, and much came from an unexpected source. William of Perth, a baker, in the course of a pilgrimage certainly to Canterbury, possibly to the Holy Land, was murdered near Rochester and buried in the cathedral. Soon there were stories of miracles and healings taking place at his tomb which resulted in pilgrims, sick and well from far and wide, flocking to the shrine. Their offerings were generous enough for the choir to be restored in 1227.

Rochester has a wealth of history. Eminent people and royalty have visited the city, but it is doubtful if any left with such unpleasant memories as did Henry VIII after his first meeting with Anne of Cleves, He referred to her as "the Flanders mare", but she was to become his fourth wife in due course.

At twelve midnight the Mail, hauled by a fresh team, left the George and its ancient vaulted cellars to drive to Chatham.

In the reign of Elizabeth I Chatham was chosen as the site for a new naval dockyard, to be further expanded in the 17th century when the Dutch threatened British supremacy of the seas. Obviously the townsfolk prefer to forget the day in 1667 when de Ruyter dared to sail up the Medway, capturing the *Royal Charles*. They prefer to recall that H.M.S. *Victory* was built and launched here in 1765.

The coach moved towards Sittingbourne through the hamlets of Rainham, Moor Street, Newington, Key Street and Chalkwell. This was the way of the Pilgrims, the road of Chaucer's *Canterbury Tales*.

Having covered almost forty miles since passing London Bridge the Dover Mail reached Sittingbourne at fifty-one minutes after midnight. The early kings of the House of Hanover enjoyed staying overnight at the Red Lion, while the rest of the party indulged at the George, Rose, Saracen's Head, Bull or White Hart.

From here the Mail left for Canterbury.

In the early years of the Dover Mail letters for the Continent were dispatched by packet to Calais. By 1794, as England was at war with France, the channel ports were closed and the packet therefore sailed between Dover and Flushing. Early the following year, according to Mr. Hasker's letters, the Mail was sent to Great Yarmouth by road, thence by packet to Cuxhaven and by road again to Hamburg. The packet office at Dover was closed, and re-opened some time after 1815.

The following arrangements existed in 1836. Every Tuesday and Friday the Dover Foreign Mail was made up at midnight, and a special coach left London for Dover, arriving just before nine o'clock. The steam packets, either *Salamander* or *Spitfire*, sailed immediately for Calais.

On other days the Dover Mail carried the foreign bags and the Calais steam packets *Ferrell, Firefly* and *Crusader* sailed on Tuesday, Wednesday, Thursday, Friday and Saturday.

The Dover Mail passed through the "garden of England", orchards of cherries, apples, pears and hops. Through villages named Radfield, Green Street, Ospringe and Preston to climb through the woods to Dunkirk and thence to Harbledown. Here stands the church of St. Nicholas, from whose tower can be seen the city of Canterbury.

They descended towards the River Stour and passed through the village of St. Dunstans and its old parish church, up a street of ancient houses, and drove beneath the postern arch of the West Gate, whose great drum towers mark the limit of the medieval city.

The Dover Mail arrived in Canterbury, stopping at the Lion in High Street, at one minute past three in the morning.

It was another inn, the Red Lion, mentioned as early as 1598, which the Duc de Nivernais, the French Ambassador, visited in September, 1762. He was on his way to London to negotiate a treaty of peace to conclude the Seven Years War, and the Red Lion was considered at that time the proper place for persons of quality to stay. For a night's lodging for twelve people, including a frugal supper of oysters, fowl, boiled mutton, poached eggs and fried whiting, including wine, the landlord presented the following bill the next morning:

	£	s.	d.
Tea, coffee and chocolate	1	4	0
Supper for self and servants	15	10	0
Bread and Beer	3	0	0
Fruit	2	15	0
Wine and punch	10	8	8
Wax candles and charcoal	3	0	0
Broken glass and china	2	10	0
Lodging	1	7	0
Tea, coffee and chocolate	2	0	0
Chaise for horses for next stage	2	16	0
£	44	10	8

The Ambassador settled the bill without any protest only remarking afterwards that "innkeepers in England must grow rich quickly".

At Rochester the following night for similar accommodation and a better meal it is recorded he was charged in the region of £3. 3s. od. News of this extraordinary bill was printed in the newspapers with the result that the landlord was ostracised by his fellow hoteliers, then by the public, and in six months he was ruined.

Around the year 600 King Ethelbert of Kent gave Augustine, missionary from Rome, a church which according to Bede was built by Roman Christians. It stood in the eastern part of the present Nave. Consecrated by Augustine it was the modest beginning of Canterbury Cathedral. In later centuries the city was captured by both Vikings and Danes, and subsequent buildings destroyed, until in 1070 the Normans commenced their cathedral. Since then, over a period of nine centuries, the work of rebuilding and restoration has continued.

Throughout these long years both kings and the common people have made their journeys to worship here. Henry II, in remorse for the action of his knights, knelt before Becket's tomb. Pilgrims followed in their thousands. Kings of England came in thanksgiving for success in their battles on French soil, and at his request the Black Prince was buried here in a tomb of his design.

King Henry VIII and the Emperor, Charles V, in 1520 paused at the shrine to "say their devotions and offer oblations", yet some eighteen years later the King appeared to have forgotten such actions. He issued a Royal Proclamation to the effect that:

> Thomas Becket, accused of being a traitor, was summoned to appear before the Court to give good reason why his shrine should not be destroyed and his name removed from the records of the English Church.

He was given thirty days to appear (having been murdered in 1170). Failure so to do meant the sentence would be pronounced against him by default. His bones would be burnt and scattered to the winds. No mention was made at this stage about spoiling the shrine, but it is recorded the Royal Commissions removed two huge chests of jewels and gold and loaded twenty-six carts with the remainder of the treasure.

His tomb might be erased but his memory remains.

Part of the glory of this great church lies in the magnificent proportions of the building and the beauty of its stained glass, but the entire conception is best expressed in Dorothy L. Sayers *The Zeal of Thy House*:

> Look then upon this Cathedral Church of Christ: imagined by men's minds, built by the labour of men's hands, working with power upon the souls of men; symbol of the everlasting Trinity, the visible temple of God.

126

Every night at three minutes past three o'clock, the Mail left Canterbury with only seventeen miles to reach its destination. The journey usually a matter of routine, the weather rarely presented any serious problems on this road, but an exception was reported in *The Times* for 2nd January, 1837:

Canterbury, 29 December

Yesterday and Tuesday large bodies of men were employed in cutting a passage through the snow on the Dover road, commencing a short distance beyond the first milestone. They have made considerable progress: and the effect of their labours is of a highly curious and interesting character. In many places the snow is 10 or 12 feet deep, filling up the entire width of the road. Through this solid mass the passage is dug away, while on each side high walls of dazzling whiteness skirt the path, looking like a range of chalk hills. Crowds of persons proceeded, during both days, to look at the novelty.

Yesterday evening they cleared away the snow as far as the turnpike. In Gutteridge bottom it lies very deep, and between the half-way house and the lane that turns off to Sibbertswould it is 10 to 12 feet deep. Whether our Dover friends are working away at their end we cannot learn; but if so, there is a chance of shaking hands with them on Barham Downs, or thereabouts, by Sunday next.

On the road to London

Nearly 400 men are employed in cutting through the snow between this city and Sittingbourne; part of them under the direction of Mr. William Clements of the Rose Inn.

Latest Particulars

The Dover mail bags were sent out on Saturday night by a steamer, which had orders to touch and leave letter bags at Margate and Ramsgate.

From this report it would seem the Dover road was not entirely cleared by Saturday, 31st December. Such a period of bad weather does not usually occur more than once in a decade, nevertheless these reports reveal the fantastic efforts made to restore the smooth passage of the Mails after such a setback.

Having discharged and picked up letter bags at Canterbury the Dover Mail was drawn swiftly by four fresh horses towards Bridge and then across Barham Down heading for the Halfway House. Although busy by day, in the early hours it was a lonely road. They had passed the up Mail and were unlikely to meet other traffic until reaching Dover. Should this happen the chances were it would have been a post-chaise carrying someone of importance who must of necessity reach London with some urgency.

The King's Messengers frequently passed this way driven fast by postillions whose orders were "not to spare the horses". As they were not expected, their arrival at an inn during the night sometimes meant waking the occupants. Cries of "Hurry, hurry in the King's name" were not unknown, and they were treated with the same respect as were the Mails.

The last change was made quickly at the Halfway House.

The Dover Mail now approached the turnpike gate at Ewell. The guard sounded his horn, the notes rang out clearly above the sound of hooves, wheels and jingling harness. They were moving fast expecting the gate to be open wide but the lights of the coach did not penetrate far. If the gate were shut it was more than likely the action of the leaders pulling up would be the first indication the coachman had. The impetus of the coach would push the wheelers forward and this could be dangerous. On such rare occasions the guard leapt down from the coach, steadied the frightened horses before he rushed to the door of the gatekeeper's lodge and banged with great severity. There would have been shouts from those on the roof of the coach. Then a light flickering in the little room above, followed by a tumbling down the stairs were indications that the gatekeeper was coming. When he appeared, possibly with a nightcap half on his head, and his breeches half pulled up, he would be greeted with oaths from guard, coachman and passengers alike. The gate unlocked, the coach passed through, and although the gatekeeper could now return to the warmth of his bed, it was unlikely he would sleep for he knew the offence would be recorded on the guard's timesheet sent back to London tomorrow. Punishment would follow – a fine of £2 – so gatekeepers did not often fail in this respect.

The Mail would make up the minutes lost quite easily on the road which descends through Buckland to reach the town itself.

For centuries Dover has been the guardian of the English Channel. High above the town stands its castle, one of the strongest and most impressive in the country. There were earlier strongholds before the great Keep and inner bailey were built by Henry II in around 1180. In the following century other monarchs extended the fortifications of the outer bailey making it one of the earliest concentric castles in the land.

The Mail drove through the town to arrive at the Post Office, New Quay, at three minutes before five o'clock in the morning. The packet was alongside waiting.

12 The Brighton Mail

In 1837, apart from the Hastings Mail, the Brighton Mail was the only two-horsed coach to leave St. Martin's-le-Grand. It was also the slowest with an average speed of just under eight miles per hour, completing the journey of fifty-five miles at twenty past three in the morning, a time hardly conducive to attract passenger traffic. First put on the road in 1791, travelling by way of East Grinstead to Brighton, it took twelve hours to reach its destination. Lack of public support resulted in the Mail being taken off for some years, and letters were carried by a stagecoach licensed for the purpose until the volume had increased to a point when it justified the Post Office to recommence its own mail service.

Unlike the roads to Exeter, York or Holyhead which were clearly defined, the road to Brighton until the end of the 18th century was one of devious ways. Most of these were merely improvements of old waggoners' tracks, and bridle ways which had been established at the whim of the travellers concerned as they made their way from place to place through mud and water.

Horace Walpole toured Sussex while on a visit to Arundel in 1749, and on his return to London wrote to his friend George Montague:

> Mr. Chute and I returned from our expedition miraculously well considering our distresses. If you love good roads, conveniences, good inns, plenty of postillions and horses, be so kind as to never go into Sussex.

As Mr. Walpole found out travel was only possible in summer and even then the post-chaise frequently overturned in deep ruts.

An advertisement appeared in the *Sussex Weekly Advertiser* on 12th May, 1756 to the effect:

> Notice is hereby given that the Lewes one day stage coach or chaise sets out from the Talbot Inn in the Borough on Saturday next the 19th inst. when likewise the Brighthelmston stage begins.
> Performed (if God permit)
> James Batchelor

It can be assumed that Mr. Batchelor was far sighted enough to put on this summer coach to attract the business beginning to develop as the result of publicity arising from Doctor Richard Russell's book *Dissertation on the use of Sea Water* published in 1752.

Russell believed it was useless to prescribe the drinking of sea-water which had been brought up from the coast and was by then stale and unpalatable. So he advised his rich constipated patients to visit Brighthelmston, a pleasant quiet hamlet on the south coast which until this time had no need of communication with the capital. Apart from drinking the waters these patients bathed in the nude and enjoyed country walks, which assisted in curing the problems arising from their idle, unhealthy London life. The fashion spread until even the Royal Family took seaside holidays, George III choosing Weymouth, while his brother, the Duke of Cumberland, preferred Brighthelmston.

In 1783 the Prince Regent, then twenty-one years old, visited his uncle. He found the relaxation he could enjoy in Brighton to his liking, so he sought a residence which resulted in his leasing a "respectable farmhouse". Later this was converted into the Pavilion.

It was not unusual for the Mails to leave London in thick fog in the winter, and then each coach was led by one or even two horsemen carrying flaming torches who slowly groped their way through the dim streets. Coachmen, outsiders and guards, well muffled up, watched the road with intense concentration as pools of light from the gas lamps loomed out of the darkness.

Contemporary writers describing London fogs referred to the smoke from the chimney pots making a soft black drizzle, which when deposited on the streets and pavements resulted in a slippery slime everywhere. Foot passengers jostling with each other frequently lost their foothold at street corners where the slime and mud was most dangerous. Pools of black water in the gutters splashed horses and pedestrians alike as carriage wheels drove through them.

The Brighton Mail crossed the Thames at Blackfriars Bridge, drove along the new Blackfriars road to the Obelisk, now St. George's Circus. They crossed into London road to reach the Elephant & Castle, a busy junction as early as the 1820s, and trotted towards Kennington with its long rows of Georgian houses. They passed the gardens of the Surrey Zoological Society which was South London's Regents Park. Over fifteen acres in extent it included a lake, Swiss chalets, grottoes, fountains, cascades, and a music hall capable of seating several thousand people. Visitors came from miles around by the 1850s, yet in the end it all disappeared in favour of streets of small terraced dwellings.

The Mail headed for Brixton, a large village in a rural setting. The little River Effa, which joined the Thames at Vauxhall, flowed on the east side of the road while the houses beyond each had their own private bridge across it. Development took place, the river disappeared into a sewer, gradually these houses were demolished to make way for a wider road, frightful terraced houses and shops.

OPPOSITE PAGE
The Brighton Mail crosses Blackfriars Bridge in fog

131

With only two horses harnessed to the coach Brixham Hill was a hard pull, but after that the going was easier as they crossed Streatham Common. In the 17th century wealthy London citizens built large houses around this common, and one was owned by Henry Thrale, a brewer from Southwick and a close friend of Doctor Johnson, who often visited him in the company of other celebrities of the time.

In 1784 Mrs. Thrale wrote to Doctor Johnson, "I write by coach the more speedily and effectually to prevent your coming hither." By coach she meant post-chaise and would have made her letter into a small parcel, as it was illegal to send ordinary letters in this way. Using this method the cost to her would have been around 2s., and it was the custom to write on the package "An extra sum will be given the porter if he deliver this immediately." This is an example of how inefficient the postal service was considered when carried by post-boys, and Streatham Common is only about eight miles from London.

Croydon in the 1830s was two towns, High Town on either side of the Brighton road stood on a ridge overlooking the older lower town which had developed besides the River Wandle. The Archbishops of Canterbury maintained a palace here for several centuries, and in the reign of Edward VI the incumbent complained that the smoke and grime associated with the burning of charcoal carried out nearby was extremely offensive. No doubt it was but even His Grace was not successful in closing down the kilns. The source of Croydon coal was the dense forests of Surrey and Sussex, supplied to London in the form of charcoal long before "sea coal" was shipped from Newcastle.

A country postmaster on this road was in the habit of rising every night to deliver the bag with its letters to the up Mail coach as it passed through the village where he lived, and once made a very unfortunate mistake. Hearing the sound of the horn, he started from his sleep, opened the window, and threw out the bag, as he thought, to the guard, who deposited what he had received in the proper place. At the next stage on the Turnpike road to London, it was discovered, that instead of the bag, the postmaster had thrown his breeches into the coach. Before this, however, the postmaster had realised the blunder he had committed, so set off with the bag, and overtaking the coach on horseback, recovered his only pair of breeches. He was glad it was still dark!

Little if any glamour surrounded the Brighton Mail, and with few passengers the coachman and guard could not grow rich on tips. Almost certainly the guard on the return journey carried fresh fish in his boot for traders in London.

The public were attracted to the many day coaches on the Brighton road, some of which were driven by amateur gentlemen, and others even by members of the aristocracy which enhanced the status of the profession and more particularly the coaches concerned. The Honourable Fred Jermingham drove the "Day Mail" (not a Royal Mail coach) and the Marquis of Worcester was a whip on the "Duke of Beaufort".

Sir St. Vincent Cotton, a gifted amateur, who after losing a very considerable fortune turned professional, drove one of the Brighton day coaches for a living. Gambling was his downfall, and a typical story is told how one evening while enjoying an excellent supper he and his friends found some maggots in the cheese. Anything that could move was considered suitable for a bet by these young bucks, so they decided on a maggot race across the table. Such was the excitement that the stakes increased dramatically during the time it took to arrange the maggots in a line for this event. Each was spurred on by its owner using a needle, and Sir Vincent's maggot looked certain to win by a good margin when in his enthusiasm he harpooned the grub. This error is believed to have cost him several thousand pounds!

After leaving Croydon the Mail trotted through the turnpike at Foxley Hatch, past Hooley House before climbing slowly over the North Downs to Merstham, whose quarries have supplied stone for London's buildings since the 12th century. They passed the Feathers Inn in Merstham, drove through the turnpike at Gatton and headed for Reigate, where they were due at ten minutes past eleven. In the time it had taken them to cover twenty-one miles the Edinburgh Mail had driven thirty-three.

Fanny Burney, who travelled through Surrey in 1779, remembered Reigate as a "very old half-ruined borough in a most neglected condition". The intensified traffic on the road brought some prosperity to the town and in particular to the Swan and the White Hart.

Crawley, the next stop, was the "half-way house" on this road and the Sun, Half Moon and George did excellent business, for in the 1830s over thirty coaches called each day. The variety of their names, each designed to attract the passengers and convince them of its particular excellence, included the Duke of Clarence, Royal George, Royal Sussex, Sovereign, Coronet, True Blue, Duke of Beaufort, Age, Comet, Rocket, Times and many others. In addition to stagecoaches there were the nobility travelling in their personal carriages, and others hiring a post-chaise, and they all needed to change horses at Crawley.

The Mail also arrived for a fresh pair at twenty minutes after midnight, when the bustle and hurry which had continued throughout the day at the George had subsided. Rowlandson painted a picture of this famous inn on a visit in 1789 showing the gallows sign stretching across the street, which is one of the few left in existence today.

To the east of the town is Crawley Down, the scene of many

historic prize-fights in Regency days, attended by thousands from all classes from the Prince Regent and his entourage to roisterers, horse-thieves and pickpockets. Every road to the venue was as thick with traffic as the roads to Epsom on Derby Day. At such contests the spectators indulged in gambling, excessive drinking, considerable rowdiness, and arguments which were usually settled with fists. In the early hours of the morning the crowds became calmer and the throng of supporters began to disperse, but many of the lanes were still blocked the next day with damaged phaetons, carriages and gigs which had collided in the dark, and many a horse was missing.

South of the town is the last remnant of the once extensive Tilgate Forest, through which the road was cut to reach Hand Cross, but the Mail had no need to change at the Red Lion here and turned left for Cuckfield. Although around 1813 a new road was opened through Bolney and Hickstead, shorter by two miles, the Mails still travelled via Cuckfield. They made their way over Stapleford Common, passed the up Mail heading for Crawley to reach Cuckfield at half-past one in the morning.

With a fresh pair of horses they turned south at Ansty Gate. The guard, sitting isolated on his perch at the rear, sometimes cold in spite of good leather boots and a bearskin rug to wrap around him, certainly had time for thoughts on these lonely stretches of road. There must have been occasions when he wondered why he had joined the service of the Post Office. Wages, half a guinea a week, which as he had to be able to read and write, were less than that of a clerk. On good routes, however, the tips could amount to £2 to £3 in a week, and he carried parcels for a fee. He often had an arrangement with provincial papers to supply them with news, also for a fee. Each year he was issued with a new uniform; he received sick pay, and could even look forward to a pension. His position carried a certain dignity, he was important in the eyes of other men. The guard must report the failure of the driver of any vehicle to give way to the Royal Mail and the Post Office sent a stern rebuke to the culprit. He must also report any tardiness on the part of gatekeepers, and any contractor who failed to provide a fresh team of fit horses on time. Sometimes he was forced to report the coachman.

They changed again at the Friar's Oak Inn, which displayed a sign with a picture of a jolly grey friar dancing beneath a huge oak tree, and proceeded towards the turnpike at Stone Pound. Passing through Clayton today there remains only one building on this stage they would recognise, the ancient church retaining part of an earlier Saxon structure. Slowly they climbed the hill from which one can see clearly two windmills known locally as Jack and Jill, and then the road cuts through a gap in the South Downs to descend to Pyecombe.

The Day coaches unlike the Mail were concerned with speed. Competition was keen with ever improving schedules, so risks had to be taken, as the fastest coaches were covering the distance in five-and-a-half hours. Minor accidents were common and did not make news, but when during the 1830s the Phoenix and Dart engaged in a race between Pyecombe and Patcham they did. The driver of the Dart was determined to pass the Phoenix and the coachman of the Phoenix equally determined to remain in the lead. Passengers in such circumstances were known to become apprehensive and this was no exception. The Dart and the Phoenix swayed, the coachmen cracked their whips continuously over the horses, who in fear galloped out of control, and when another frightened team came alongside, they panicked. The wheels of the coaches became interlocked, the respective teams entangled, and the lurching coaches finally overturned. Luggage and occupants were hurled in all directions ending with broken bones, sore heads, injured horses, damaged coaches and two disillusioned coachmen. In the slang of the profession "a bad case".

The Brighton Mail arrived safely at the Post Office, New Road, at twenty minutes past three in the morning and did not leave again for London until half-past ten that evening.

13 The Holyhead Mail

Through St. Albans to Birmingham

It was evening on Tuesday, 20th June, 1837, and the crowds waiting beyond the railing of the Post Office building in St. Martin's le Grand were silent. There nineteen coaches were drawn up ready to leave at eight o'clock, with most of the coachmen already on the box and guards supervising the last of the letter bags being loaded. They all wore black arm-bands, and the coaches were decked with laurel wreaths as a mark of respect. That morning King William IV had died, and his niece the Princess Victoria had acceded to the throne. Unknown to them it was the passing of an era.

The first news that there was a queen on the throne of Great Britain again would be carried by the Mail coach to Holyhead and thence to Ireland. No-one living in the country could remember a queen as the monarch. People knew very little about the Princess Victoria, apart from the fact that she was seventeen years of age and lived with her mother, the Duchess of Kent, in Kensington Palace. Rarely had she been seen at any royal event.

At eight o'clock all was ready, ostlers whipped off the horse-cloths, and the coaches moved forward to the noise of the horses' hooves and commands from each coachman to his team, as they filed out of the gateway opposite the Bull & Mouth. They were bound for Halifax, Leeds, Manchester, Chester, Glasgow, Liverpool and Holyhead.

The guard of the leading coach frequently sounded his horn. "Clear the way" as the Mails trotted through Newgate Street, turned up Giltspur Street, towards the Old Smithfield Market. Early in the 19th century this was the largest cattle market in Europe, but because of its revolting stench and filth there were constant plans for its removal to a site outside the city.

The coaches moving in a line wheeled into St. John's Street. Here was Hicks Hall, although no building actually now exists. Its importance was the fact that from this point all the roads to the north-west of the country were measured.

The Mails moved up St. John's Street – the guards still sounding their horns, which echoed through the narrow streets. Oncoming traffic, whether post-chaise, omnibus, or stage waggon, must pull to one side. There was no question of keeping to the left – everyone drove on the centre of the road. A solitary lamp lighter made his way along the pavements, on his nightly task.

At the top of St. John's Street, on the opposite side of the road stood the Angel, well frequented by drovers and carriers for the market, and a few yards further on the Cock (or Peacock). Here many stagecoaches called to pick up passengers.

The stones of the city's paved streets gave way to a country lane before the coaches reached Islington Green. Around the Green were the church, some houses and a few farms which supplied milk for the capital. Soon all this would be swallowed up when London broke through the confines of the new city road.

As the line of coaches trotted through the village of Holloway none had thoughts of prisons. The leading coach was the Halifax Mail, and the coachman was watching ahead, towards the turn-pike at the end of the village. He was listening for the approach of the Shrewsbury Wonder – one of the most famous stagecoaches of its time. The up coach left Shrewsbury at five o'clock in the morn-ing and covered the 153 miles to London to arrive at the Bull & Mouth at nine o'clock the same evening. It did not pause at the turnpike as certain of the larger contractors, like Sherman, had agreed with the turnpike authorities to pay their tolls each month. This gave them a decided advantage in speed. The Mails paid no tolls so the gate remained open for them.

Highgate, as the name implies, was a gate on a hill, which from time immemorial had been the tollgate of the Bishop of London. The steepness of the road through the village for a long time caused great inconvenience to traffic, so a decision was made to by-pass it. The plans drawn up were for a new road on the north-eastern side of the village which tunnelled through the hill and rejoined the Great North Road between the fifth and sixth milestones. This great undertaking was commenced in 1810 but two years later a section of the tunnel collapsed. Fortunately no-one was injured. It was decided to create an open road with a greatly reduced gradient and to construct a viaduct to carry Hornsey Lane over the new highway, giving it the appearance of a modern motorway. Arch-way Road, as the new highway was called, was opened in August, 1813, and the Holloway turnpike removed to the foot of the Arch-way itself. From Hornsey Lane as it crossed the Arch was a won-derful view of London which became a great attraction for visitors. It also became renowned as a place for frequent suicides!

The new road rejoined the older one, crossed Finchley Common, once a favourite place for the activities of highwaymen, and pro-ceeded via the hamlet of Whetstone to climb up Barnet Hill.

Robert Southey described a view from the top of a coach in *Letters from Espriella*:

The sun was setting, and the long twilight of an English summer evening gave the English landscape a charm wholly its own. As soon as it grew dark the coach lights were lighted. Starlight and mild summer air made the situation not unpleasant.

Remarkably he made no mention of the dust!

There were three extensive inns in Barnet, the Red Lion, Green

*The Highgate Arch
from the Holloway
Turnpike*

Man and Mitre. Between eleven and seventeen minutes past nine, seven Mails required to change horse here. The post office at Barnet in 1835 had become responsible for the handling of bye-bags resulting in a further loading of mail in the box beneath the guard. It is not difficult to imagine the feverish activity during these six minutes. As well as the bags, twenty-eight fresh horses had to be "put to" and twenty-eight led back to the stalls. During this time a stage from the north or a noble person in his own carriage heading for town might arrive. They would have to wait.

The news of the king's death was given to the ostlers and in a matter of minutes came the cry from each coachman "Let 'em go", and the ostlers released the heads of the excited horses and they were away.

The Glasgow and Leeds Mails took the Welwyn road out of the town, the rest kept to the Holyhead road which passes through Hadley Green. Here is a memorial to serve as a reminder of Easter Sunday, 1471, when Edward IV and his troops marched out of Barnet to meet and defeat his adversary the Earl of Warwick.

The descent from Barnet to South Minns allowed a fresh team to make up any lost time. Each evening five coachmen drove their teams fast up Ridge Hill to cover as quickly as possible the last stretch of road between Colney and St. Albans. It was so exposed that they dreaded it in winter, for gales or driving snow here often meant delays. On this June night they had no anxiety.

After the great blizzard on Christmas Day, 1836, the down Manchester Mail overturned here. On this same road in 1820, the Chester and Holyhead Mails were overturned in a collision and one passenger killed. The coachman of the Holyhead Mail was at the time overtaking the one bound for Chester, and it is recorded that both coachmen were driving recklessly. The inquest held at the Peahen, St. Albans, found them guilty of manslaughter. They were sent for trial and imprisoned.

The Halifax Mail was the first of the seven to reach the Peahen at St. Albans, and once again told of the king's death.

The Romans called this town, standing on the banks of the River Ver, Verulamium. It was Alban, one of their soldiers, who gave the town its present name. He was put to death for sheltering a fellow-Christian. Later he was canonised becoming Britain's first Christian martyr, and a shrine was erected at the place where he was executed on the hill above Verulamium. The Saxons built a monastery around the shrine, the Normans rebuilt it, and Henry VIII destroyed it. The abbey church remained and was sold by Edward VI to the town for £400. The church, which became a cathedral in 1887, is over 550 feet in length, one of the longest in England. The Norman red-bricked tower remains together with the choir, transepts and eastern bays of the nave. In the 13th century the nave was extended adding to the variety of architectural work in this imposing building. Meanwhile the town grew up around the abbey itself.

In the days of the coaches St. Albans abounded in inns. Holywell Hill was just one long street of them, which included the White Hart, George, Saracen's Head, Angel, Dolphin, Red Lion, Peahen, with many others.

Nostalgia for coaching times must have lingered in St. Albans as in 1882 a stagecoach named "The Wonder" was put on the road to run daily to London, and it continued on this route until around 1900.

The steep descent of Romeland and Fishpool Street to the village of St. Michaels had been a problem for a long time when in 1826 Thomas Telford was consulted. With his usual boldness he cut an entirely new road with an easy gradient to a point some two miles near Redbourne called Fishponds.

Redbourne, with its Georgian and Queen Anne red-bricked houses is only four-and-a-half miles from St. Albans, but the Mails changed again at the Black Bull at sixteen minutes before eleven to enable them to tackle the pull up to the summit of the Chilterns with a fresh team.

From Redbourne to Dunstable is just over eight miles. A lonely road, and only the straggling village of Markyate Street could boast of an inn if required. For the nervous passenger some comfort might be had from the fact that there were five coaches travelling more or less together and highwaymen were less frequent than they had been a few decades previously. Still there were rumours that ghosts of nuns could be seen in the park of Markyate Cell, once a 12th century priory. There was also the memory of Lady Ferrers who had lived in this house, rebuilt after its dissolution. Disguised as a man she robbed the coaches on this isolated road. No-one suspected her until she was shot dead and her true identity revealed.

Earlier than the exploits of Lady Ferrers another "worked" this road – the renowned "Gentleman Harry". Harry Simms was an undergraduate at Cambridge but left to enlist in the Army. He deserted but was unlucky enough to be pressganged into the Navy. He deserted yet again and became a highwayman. His last hold-up was on this road. He robbed three travellers and allowed them to continue their journey towards Dunstable, while he waited to rob the Warrington Stage. The next day he was recognised at an inn in Dunstable but easily escaped and rode to Hockcliffe. Drink was then his downfall, for that evening he was arrested in a drunken stupor and taken to London under escort. After his trial he was hanged at Tyburn.

As the pace of the horses quickened at the start of the descent to Dunstable, there was always some passenger aboard who sighed with relief!

140

Almost everyone changed horses at Dunstable. The Halifax Mail arrived at twenty-one minutes past eleven followed by the other four between eleven and thirteen minutes later. Apart from the Mails many stagecoaches pulled up at either the Red Lion, the Saracen's Head, Crown, Sugarloaf or Swan.

Between half-past eight and noon each day the following stage coaches stopped at Dunstable:

The Wonder, Stag and Nimrod for Shrewsbury.

For Birmingham, Tally Ho, Independent Tally Ho and Economist.

The Hope bound for Halifax and the Times for Nottingham.

For Leeds the Express and Courier. For Leicester the Union.

Driving to Liverpool were the Albion and Umpire, and to Manchester the Telegraph, Red Rover, Royal Defiance, Royal Bruce, and Beehive.

The Augustine Priory at Dunstable was founded in the early part of the 12th century. In 1533 Archbishop Cranmer held a court in the Lady Chapel to consider the application by the king for a divorce. He summoned Catherine of Aragon, then staying at Ampthill, to appear before him. She refused. The marriage was then declared null and void, and Cranmer pinned the notice of divorce on the priory door. A few years later the priory was dissolved and only the nave, now the parish church, remains.

In the last few days of December, 1836, a blizzard left conditions so bad they were remembered for more than one generation.

The Times, Monday, 2nd January, 1837, quotes:

A gentleman who left Sheffield by the Hope coach of Sunday week reports that the coach did not complete its journey till Saturday afternoon. Between Nottingham and Mansfield, they came up with three coaches blocked in the snow. There was only a labourer's cottage for miles around in which the passengers had sought shelter. It was a place with only one chamber above, and where ginger beer and cakes were sold. In all 16 passengers were assembled here with the prospect of staying several days. Fortunately, a pig had just been killed by the cottagers, so that the supply of meat was good, but then there was scarcely any bread in the house, or hope of getting it. At places around the snow was lying nine foot deep. The Hope left Mansfield with eight horses, and was drawn into Nottingham with 10. At one place they picked up a poor boy nearly perished with cold. The boy was got up by a gentleman jumping down from behind, while the coach was still moving, for the coachman declared he could not come to a dead stop, as if he did he would not be able to get the wheels in motion afterwards.

This coach passed through Dunstable sometime in the early hours of the Saturday morning – six days after leaving Halifax!

To reduce the gradient on the road from Dunstable to Hockcliffe, Telford cut through the chalk and used the spoil to achieve this. He also engineered an extensive drainage scheme to carry away the water from Dunstable Downs to the south and the Brickhills to the north. Prior to this, as Celia Fiennes relates in *Journeys of Celia Fiennes*, published in 1697, it was:

> Seven miles over a sad road, called Hockley-in-ye-Hole, as full of deep slows in ye winter it must have been Empassable.

Since Roman times Watling Street must have deteriorated considerably when this lady made her journey!

Hockcliffe grew in importance in the coaching era, standing as it did at the junction of the Manchester, and the Birmingham, Shrewsbury and Holyhead roads. Only nine years after Celia Fiennes' writings the road was turnpiked.

At twelve minutes past midnight, having covered thirty-seven miles, the Halifax Mail passed the White Hart at Hockcliffe and took the road for Woburn.

Near Hockcliffe in 1835 two serious accidents are recorded, and doubtless there were others. The Hope, a stagecoach from Halifax, got out of control on the hill near Battlesden House, and all the passengers were seriously injured. Later the Shrewsbury Greyhound also overturned with similar results. In the 1830s not only were there many more coaches on the road by day, but fierce competition between the operators often resulted in coachmen taking chances to keep to their tight schedules.

The Mails had a much better record than the stagecoaches, but, usually due to weather, even they met with the odd accident. On Boxing Day, 1836 all five Mails were halted near Hockcliffe stuck in deep snowdrifts. Finally they managed to release the up Holyhead Mail, placed all the bags from the other coaches in it, instead of passengers, and with a team of eight cart horses struggled on towards London.

Both the Liverpool and Holyhead Mails cantered on through the darkness of the night towards Fenny Stratford. Behind them Manchester and Chester took the Woburn road at the Hockcliffe turnpike.

The Holyhead road continues to follow the course of the older Watling Street and climbs over the Brickhills. After changing horse at Little Brickhill the coach descended to the valley of the River Ouse.

The Mails rattled through Fenny Stratford making more noise than the Fenny poppers. This ceremony of firing the "poppers" near the church of St. Martins on the anniversary of its dedication (November 11th) is still maintained. The gunmetal "Quart" pots are filled with powder and fired with the touch of a heated iron rod.

Sleep must have been a problem in Fenny Stratford. Just before one o'clock in the morning these two Mails thundered through on their way to Stoney Stratford. At about a quarter to two the up Liverpool coach passed heading for Hockcliffe to be followed just after two o'clock by the up Holyhead Mail, also dashing towards Hockcliffe.

It was a good galloping ground for the next six miles and before 1838 the coaches rushed past an insignificant country inn called the Pig and Whistle. In April of that year the London to Birmingham Railway was opened to this point and a temporary station erected by the roadside. The Pig and Whistle was immediately raised to the status of the Denbigh Hall. From here passengers from London were taken by coach to Rugby, a distance of thirty-eight miles, to resume their train journey to Birmingham. The coach traffic was really more than the place could cope with, but the arrangement continued until 17th September, when the line was opened entirely from London to Birmingham. Within a few weeks Denbigh Hall had lapsed back into obscurity.

The two main inns at Stoney Stratford are the Cock and the Bull, which stand at different ends of the town. Coaching gossip gleaned at one, when compared with the version at the other, deviated so much that it became known as a "Cock and Bull story".

The Mails pulled up outside the Cock at twenty-six minutes past one.

They had driven over fifty-two miles in five-and-a-half hours. Here the coachman who had brought the Mail from London gave over the reins to another who would take the coach to Birmingham. Five minutes was allowed here, as the timesheet expressed it, for "Business".

The guard called the passengers to rejoin the coach. The new coachman after checking the harnessing of the fresh team mounted the box. Everyone aboard, a shout to the ostlers, and they were off.

In the summer of 1838 there were alterations to these Mails which then started and finished their respective journeys at Denbigh Hall, and not St. Martin's le Grand. The railway was taking over the task of carrying some of Her Majesty's Mails. Later that year the Liverpool coach was taken off the road, and the Holyhead started from Birmingham. A change then came over the Stratfords; they became silent. The inns empty, the horses sold, and the stables deserted. For several generations the inhabitants had spent their lives working in the coaching business. It disappeared in a matter of months resulting in great hardship.

But in 1837 these Mails still crossed the long causeway and bridge over the River Ouse, and cantered along the level road to Towcester taking just forty minutes to cover the eight miles between these two towns.

On the outskirts of Towcester is Easton Neston, a dignified and gracious building which was the work of Nicholas Hawksmoor. As a young man he was Wren's master draughtsman in the building of Greenwich and St. Paul's. In Towcester the Saracen's Head (later renamed the Pomfret Arms) was the principal inn. There was no crowd of idlers, such as those who greeted Mr. Pickwick, when the Mails changed at twelve minutes past two in the morning.

On Telford's improved road the Liverpool and Holyhead coaches passed through Forster's Booth, across the Grand Junction Canal, and at Weedon Beck left the line of the old Watling Street, turning west for Daventry.

The Mails did not enter this town, once famous for the making of whips, but travelled along Sheaf Street to the Wheatsheaf Posting and Excise Office. Bags were dropped, fresh horses harnessed, and as dawn was breaking on this June morning the coaches were on their way to Dunchurch, carrying their sad news yet further.

Liverpool and Holyhead Mails, still together, climbed Falconer's Hill to reach Dunchurch at eleven minutes past four. The hostelries included the Black Dog, Dun Cow, Blue Boar, Red Lion and the Green Man. Drunkenness was punished here by six hours in the stocks, and a fine of 5s. This bye-law must have been relaxed when, after the great blizzard of December, 1836, the passengers of many stranded coaches gathered in the town and carried on their Christmas festivities in two nights of revelling!

From Dunchurch to Whitley Common is a good level road, and the Mails moved quickly on this stage, but their times did not compete with some of the Birmingham Day Coaches. Harry Tresslove, coachman of the Independent Tally Ho, always galloped the entire five mile stage between Dunchurch and the Black Dog, Stretton upon Dunsmore, in eighteen minutes, an average of seventeen miles per hour! Here he changed his exhausted horses in just over a minute and galloped on with a fresh team into Coventry.

In the narrow streets it was difficult to manoeuvre past other vehicles. They made their way up Much Park Street, Earl Street, and High Street, passed the 14th century Guildhall of St. Mary, with its minstrel gallery. Outsiders saw the slender spire of the parish church of St. Michael (given cathedral status in 1919) most of which was destroyed by enemy action in 1940.

Throughout the Civil War, Coventry was one of Cromwell's strongholds, and Royalists captured over a wide area were "sent to Coventry" and imprisoned in the church of St. John, where there was no chance of outside sympathy.

At eighteen minutes past five both Mails left the King's Head by way of Smithford and Fleet Street to ascend Windmill Hill, the vantage point from which Turner painted a picture of Coventry.

Six miles to Meriden, the village cross claims to stand on the exact centre of England. On their arrival at Stone Bridge a further change of horses, and before they left yet another hamlet had heard the news of the new queen.

The Liverpool Mail left to make its way via Coleshill and Litch-field and would complete its journey at ten minutes to five that afternoon. Holyhead was still a distance of 160 miles, taking a further seventeen hours to reach the town.

Now alone, the Holyhead Mail moved quickly through Wells Green to approach the outskirts of Birmingham, whose 106,000 inhabitants in 1828 were not represented by a single Member of Parliament. Down these streets at around seven o'clock in the morning outsiders had glimpses into first floor windows, and housemaids were already washing the steps. They passed shops where boys were taking down the shutters, and from pastry-makers came a pleasant smell of baking which reminded those on the coach they would soon stop for breakfast. Early morning traffic was on the streets, the guard standing up sounded his horn "Clear the way" for the Royal Mail. Dogs and urchins scurried out of the way of the moving coach. Street carts pulled to one side as the Mail swept towards the Bull Ring, while the guard called to no-one in particular "The King is dead – Long live the Queen."

At eight minutes past seven they pulled up at the Swan in High Street. Quickly a crowd gathered to hear the news. In just over eleven hours they had driven 109 miles.

14 The Holyhead Mail

Birmingham through Shrewsbury and Bangor to Holyhead

The Holyhead Mail waited at the Swan for thirty-five minutes. Everyone was ready for breakfast, in fact there were those who nearly fell off the coach in their eagerness. Male passengers feeling the need of a shave called for the barber, to be followed by as much breakfast as time allowed. The menu usually consisted of coffee or tea, roll and butter, ham and eggs, tongue, cold beef or pigeon pie with porter. It was a "free for all", accompanied with pushing, shoving and shouting for waiters, with perhaps the odd gentleman quietly looking after the lady passengers.

From Birmingham, situated almost in the centre of England, the canal system in the early 19th century was so well developed it was possible to reach the navigable sections of the Mersey, Severn, Trent and Thames. This was essential for a town known as the "Workshop of England", to enable the import of the coal and raw materials it required and then to export its goods, proudly marked "Made in Birmingham", to customers all over the world. At the beginning of 1837 more than 300 coaches arrived and departed from the five principal inns, the Albion, Castle and Swan in High Street, the Saracen's Head in Bull Street and the Hen and Chickens (nicknamed "The Fowls") in New Street.

De Quincey stayed frequently at the Hen and Chickens and wrote:

> Never did I sleep there but I had reason to complain that the discreet hen did not gather her flock to roost at less variable hours. Till two or three in the morning I was kept waking by those retiring, and about three commenced the morning functions of the porter, or of boots or under boots who began their rounds for collecting the several freights for the Highflyer, or the Tally-ho, or the Bang-up to all points of the compass, and too often (as must happen in such immense establishments) blundered into my room with that appalling "Now Sir – the horses are coming out!" So that rarely indeed have I happened to sleep in Birmingham.

The businessmen of Birmingham were looking ahead. By the end of the next year, 1838, the railway, only planned some five years previously, would connect their town with the capital, and also with both Liverpool and Manchester. Trains could average about twenty miles per hour, twice the speed of the coaches. At the General Post Office in London they were quick to realise the advantages of the transfer of the mails to the faster and cheaper

146

railways. Neither were coach proprietors all over the country slow to adjust to necessary change.

BRISTOL MERCURY 1st July 1837

NIBLETT'S ROYAL MAIL AND GENERAL

COACH OFFICE, BROAD ST. BRISTOL

In consequence of the intended opening of the Railroad from Birmingham to Liverpool on Tuesday next 4th July I. NIBLETT has made arrangements for the Birmingham Coaches to leave his Establishment at an early hour in the morning, and to arrive in Birmingham in time for passengers to proceed by train direct to Liverpool the same day.

This advertisement naturally made no mention of the discomforts of early rail travel. First class was similar to sitting in a coach except there were six inside instead of the four on the Mails. Second class was an open carriage, but had an awning to protect passengers slightly from the rain and red hot cinders and smoke from the engine. Third class passengers stood in an open truck. Everyone experienced the heavy jolting from rails placed on granite slabs and suffered the continuous and deafening rattle. Tunnels were particularly unpleasant. For those who appreciated it, there was the thrill of speeds up to thirty miles per hour downhill! First class fares were around three-quarters of the cost of inside on a coach, but third class "mixed with goods" was only half that charged on the stage for outsiders.

The Holyhead Mail was due to leave the Swan at forty-three minutes after seven.

There never seemed enough time to eat a reasonable meal, which doubtless suited the innkeepers better than the passengers. All too soon was the call "Time's up gentlemen, all aboard the coach." Often passengers stuffed rolls into their pockets, paid the bill, around 2s., tipped the waiter and still hungry rejoined the coach.

Although Dr. Johnson stated that "insiders were people who pretended they were socially greater than they were", obviously it was not always the case. Parson Woodforde made a number of coach journeys recording among his fellow passengers, an officer in the Guards, a civil servant on business, a lady and her two daughters visiting relatives. On one occasion he writes that the other occupants were "a very fat woman with a dog and many band boxes, which incommoded us, and also a poor sickly old man". Another reference refers to a stout man who was a grocer, two female servants of a nobleman whose manservant travelled outside.

*Breakfast at the
Swan,
Birmingham*

One can imagine that conversation was on the same lines as today, with four people crammed into the interior of the coach. It was usually stuffy, and provided little or no view of the countryside through which they were passing. On this journey their remarks must have centred around the reign of the late king, who was exceedingly popular and the almost unknown young Princess Victoria.

A fresh team, a new coachman and guard, and the Mail eased itself away from the Swan still surrounded by curious crowds. They trotted up Bull Street, Snow Hill and Hockley Hill. From this higher ground looking back was a view of the spire of St. Martin's Church set amidst tall buildings with numerous small chimney pots, and surrounded by a forest of smoking stacks of the foundries. Above them a pall of black smoke hung in the morning air.

The next hour of their journey over an uninteresting road took them through Sandwell Green, Bromwich Heath, and Wednesbury. Between Moxley and Billston the coachman might mention to his companion on the box seat that shortly they would meet the up Shrewsbury Wonder due in town that evening. This item of interest was sometimes passed to the other outsiders to be followed by an air of expectation and mild excitement. The stagecoach approached resplendent in yellow and black drawn by four spirited horses. Coachmen working this ground knew each other well, they collected their respective teams to a controlled trot, saluted with their whips as they passed, and the guard of the Mail shouted his news as the coaches accelerated again in opposite directions.

The Holyhead Mail drove towards Wolverhampton. Both the Swan in High Green (now Queen's Square) and the Lion in North Street could only be approached through narrow streets, so the Mails changed at the Hotel, Cocks Street at one minute past nine o'clock, leaving by way of Barn Street (now Salop Street) and right away for Chapel Ash, and the open country again.

Up Tettenhill, through the Wergs to the summit of Summerhouse Hill could be a pleasant ride on a sunny June morning. Here was an inn referred to in the old time sheets as Summerhouses, where another change was made.

The next stop was Shifnal, described in *The Old Curiosity Shop*:

They passed a large church, and in the streets were a number of old houses, built of a kind of earth or plaster, crossed and re-crossed in a great many directions with black beams, which gave them a remarkable ancient look. The doors too were arched and low, some with oaken portals and quaint benches, where the former inhabitants had sat on summer evenings. The windows were latticed in little diamond panes that seemed to "wink and blink".

No reference is made of the elegant Georgian buildings in this town, maybe they were too modern to be worth a mention.

At fourteen minutes past ten the Holyhead Mail stopped at the Jerningham Arms. While the horses were changed, they briefly gave the news to onlookers. Then they were off towards Wellington.

Coaches on this route did not enter the town of Wellington but after rejoining the course of Watling Street turned at Cock's Corner for Haygate. Certain coachmen drew attention to a cone shaped hill to the south of the road which rises to nearly 1,400 feet known as the Wrekin. From its summit are astonishing views in every direction. Northwards the Cheshire plain and to the north-east Axe Edge and the High Peak of Derbyshire. To the south-east and south, the Lickey Hills and the Clee Hills near Ludlow. South-west is the Long Mynd, and to the north-west the mountains of Llangollen through which the Mail must travel. They lit a beacon on the Wrekin to warn of the coming of the Armada.

The Haygate Inn was the last stop before Shrewsbury, and instructions on the Way-bill read: "Bags dropt here for, and taken up from Wellington."

The new team kept up an exciting pace as the road descends to Norton and down to the River Severn. They came to Atcham Bridge built in 1768, an imposing seven-arched structure, which always proved difficult to manoeuvre with a coach and four horses.

Four miles to Shrewsbury, the Mail crossed the English bridge. Constructed in 1774 it stands now unused while 20th century traffic roars over a modern structure. The old milestone beside the original bridge still exists reading: "London 147m, Shifnall 14m, Salop 3m. 6f". The Mail now turned to climb the steep lane called Wyle Cop.

It was a minute before twelve noon when they stopped at the Lion. There were always onlookers at this time of day, errand boys wasting their masters' time, old men who had seen it all before, and those meeting or saying farewell to travellers. This day they were told the news, a new queen, and doubtless somebody sent for the town crier.

The Lion is one of the few great coaching houses remaining today. The owner of this inn in 1825 was Isaac Taylor, who with E. Sherman in London put the "Shrewsbury Wonder" on the road. To sustain its daily performance, the most reliable jobmasters were required to horse it, which included two of Taylor's brothers at Haygate and Shifnal. A stud of over 150 excellent horses, possibly Clevelands, were maintained specially for this coach. Being expensive animals at a cost of at least £30 each, they only worked two hours in twenty-four including the reverse stage. For nine years no Day coach dared to rival the "Wonder", but in 1834 Benjamin Horne, realising this was a profitable route, put the Nimrod on the

The up Holyhead
Mail leaves the
Lion, Shrewsbury

same road. An advertisement in the *Shrewsbury Chronicle* in July, 1835 was Taylor's reply:

> Isaac Taylor, ever grateful for the distinguished support he has received from the public, announces a new and elegant fast day coach, called the "STAG", every morning at a ¼ bef. 5 morn. arriving at the Bull & Mouth at seven the same evening. Isaac Taylor has been induced to commence running the "STAG" to prevent the celebrated "WONDER" being in any way injured by racing or at all interfered with in the regularity which has hitherto been observed.

Sherman and Taylor timed the Stag to run ahead of the Nimrod, which Horne had purposely placed ahead of the Wonder. Fares were cut in fierce competition, and there were accidents involving the Nimrod before it was taken off the road. The Wonder continued for many years until eventually it gave way to the trains. Long after this there were still people in Shrewsbury who would relate how Sam Haywood, who drove the Wonder from the Hen & Chickens, Birmingham, completed this journey. Wyle Cop and the notorious entrance to the Lion yard presented no problems for him for he took the hill at a full canter, reined in, and executed the neatest of turns to pass under the archway to the yard at a trot, "feather edging it" with only an inch or so to spare.

Five minutes passed quickly. A new coachman, a change of some passengers, and the eager horses drew the coach away to head for Oswestry.

Leaving the town by way of the Welsh bridge the Mail hastened through Shelton, crossed the Montford Bridge, and cantered towards Nesscliff, where the team harnessed at Shrewsbury were replaced.

A few miles further along the road stands one of the most unusual signposts in England – Ruyton of the Eleven Towns. Ruyton was an amalgamation of eleven hamlets and granted a charter for a market in 1308. In the next century a decision was made in favour of the market at Oswestry, and Ruyton still remained a village.

Near Twyford Cross the up and down Holyhead Mails passed.

It was a quarter to two when the Mail called at the Cross Keys and Queen's Head, Oswestry.

The Queen's Head remains as the Queen's Hotel but the Cross Keys which used to adjoin this property has disappeared in the construction of a new road.

The news caused considerable excitement in the town, and the coach departing a minute or so late had to force its way through the crowd. Apart from the descent to Chirk Bridge crossing the River Ceiriog the next stage of the road is level and elevated giving those on top of the coach some fine views. At the turnpike gate at Whitehurst the road starts to turn westwards into the valley of the River Dee or the Vale of Llangollen depending upon one's ancestry.

About four miles to the north is Wynnstay Park – once the home of Sir William Watkins-Wynne. For thirty years he transferred annually the rents collected from his considerable estate to his bankers in London. Most landed gentry of his standing possessed a Fourgon. It was a carriage used to transport the servants and luggage which proceeded ahead of their own chariot when travelling. He gave orders that this vehicle, half carriage and half van, should be given an iron bullet-proof lining and before each journey to London must be completely overhauled. Then in the company of his four strongest gamekeepers, each armed with a loaded double-barrelled hammer gun, he set off. The luggage compartment loaded with silver and gold would have been sufficient to tempt any highwayman. Precautions against this possibility were made in great detail, travelling only by day about fifty miles, and staying at well-known and trusted inns. While Sir William slept in a comfortable feather bed, his stalwart gamekeepers, two at a time, stood guard over the vehicle with the two carriage dogs which accompanied them. Even in these dangerous times they were never once threatened.

The Mail arrived outside the King's Head at Llangollen at three minutes to three in the afternoon.

In the early days of this road the town was notorious for its bad inns. There were only two of any consequence, the Hand and the King's Head (later the Royal Hotel). The Irish patriot, Daniel O'Connell, who travelled frequently over this road, knew both and in the mid-1820s when the standard of service at the King's Head had improved, he wrote in the visitors' book:

I remember this village with very bad cheer
Ere the Ladies, God bless them, set this inn here.
But the traveller now is sure of good fare
Let him stay at this inn or go to that 'ere
But all who can read will sure understand
How vastly superior's the HEAD to the HAND.

The reference to the "Ladies" is to the renowned "Ladies of Llangollen". Presumably their distinguished visitors, which included the Duke of Wellington, Sir Walter Scott, Wordsworth, and many others, coupled with increased trade on the improved road, had raised the standard of the King's Head.

Ahead, the most difficult part of the journey, fifty-three miles of mountain roads including the Nant Ffrancon Pass. First suggested in 1800 as a shorter alternative to the route via Chester and Conway, this road was poorly constructed, and after a few years considered dangerous. In 1810 Thomas Telford was appointed to survey the entire length of the road to Bangor, in his report to the Treasury the estimated cost was £394,480. Gradually over the next ten years the road was vastly improved. The fact that after the Act of Union many Irish Members of Parliament had to travel between Dublin and Westminster certainly brought pressure to bear on the authorities to construct and maintain a good road.

From the King's Head, Llangollen, which is 300 feet above sea level, the Mail travelled along a road which follows the course of the river valley. From this elevated position there was a glimpse through the trees of the beautiful yet artificial Horse-shoe falls at a point where the river turns around the high ground of Rhysgog. Here they climbed to a height of 560 feet before descending again to Glyn-Dyfrdwy, where having covered only five miles they changed the tired horses and made for Corwen (500 feet).

At three minutes to four they pulled up at the New Inn, where twenty-eight minutes were allowed for dinner. During this time the bags for Ireland were transferred to a waiting coach which had brought the up mail from Holyhead in the morning. A fresh coachman and guard took over, and it is likely they were Welsh speaking.

At twenty-five minutes past four they left with six horses, crossed the River Alwen, and then commenced the stiff climb to Tyn-yn-ant (782 feet). Three changes in fifteen miles taking just over a minute each time enabled them to maintain their speed. The ostlers had the new horses ready on the road; in summer their task was easy, but in winter it was dark when the Mail left Corwen resulting in all the changes on this mountain road being carried out by the dim lights of the coach and the odd lantern.

The fresh horses were put to as the coachman watched from the box. They were off to a sharp trot but still they had to climb. It was a lonely road, the moors sweeping gradually upwards towards the distant mountains. A few isolated cottages and, very rarely, a drover moving his black cattle along the road. When this occurred, the guard leapt to his feet and gave a long blast on his horn. At least it relieved the boredom and was fun to watch the cattle scatter! No longer could it be said: "Guards on the Irish road shooting at dogs, hogs, sheep and poultry as they passed". An Act of Parliament in 1811 forbade the firing of their weapons except in self-defence, but the fine must have been the deterrent, a maximum £5, although the Post Office in *Instructions to Guards* quoted £2.2s.0d. – but still four weeks' wages!

The coachman spoke only to the horses, for he had to use all his skill to obtain the best from the team, as with their shoulders hard into their collars they strained to keep the coach moving. They reached Cerrig-y-Druidion (Rock of the Druids) and still they

154

climbed. At last at Glasfryn, 908 feet above sea level, the ascent was over. To mark the summit a few scattered houses and a derelict tollhouse.

Within a mile was Cernioge, the name they had seen on every milestone since Corwen. It was a large posting house which today has disappeared. The time twenty-one minutes to six. The weary horses which had hauled the coach (weighing overall about 2 tons) up from Tyn-y-ant could rest. A fresh team would take over the ten mile stage through Pentre Foelas down to Bettys-y-coed. Experienced horses were required, the wheelers in particular strong enough to hold the coach on its long descent. Finally they crossed Telford's Waterloo Bridge to drive into the town itself. Here is the Royal Oak, once a favourite hostelry of David Cox, a celebrated landscape artist. There is always the sound of rushing water in Bettys-y-coed.

Having harnessed six strong horses at New Stables they faced the climb to Capel Curig, only seven miles but an ascent of over 500 feet. Their road passed above the Swallow falls, over Tyhyll Bridge, and through Pont-cyfyn, upwards all the way to pause at Capel Curig Inn at two minutes past seven. The exhausted sweating horses were led away from the coach, and six fresh ones harnessed, for from here the ascent continues to the 1,000 feet contour line.

About a mile short of Llyn Ogwen the two extra horses were released to return back with their rider, and the Holyhead Mail commenced the descent to Bangor.

The scenery is one of awesome splendour with the high mountains of Carnedd Dafydd on one side, the range of the Glyders on the other, and the Nant Ffrancon pass dark in their shadows.

They reached Tyn-y-maes at fourteen minutes to eight o'clock and left to drive further down the pass beside the restless River Ogwen tumbling towards the sea.

Smartly they trotted through the High Street of the city of Bangor, whose cathedral was then in a deplorable condition. The thoughts of those on the coach must have been that the worst of their journey was over, certainly after 1826 when they could cross the Menai Bridge instead of the hazardous ferry to Anglesey. The Irish Members of Parliament may have felt differently however. They must have possessed great stamina, for the ride of twenty-seven hours on the coach was now to be followed by a seven hour sea crossing to Howth, before they set foot on Irish soil.

The Mail halted at the Penryn Arms hotel. Belonging to the Bicknell family who maintained a "special team of four spicey greys to horse the Mails". Now part of Bangor University, it was a large fashionable establishment of 190 beds, described as "the equal of anything in the Metropolis". They employed eighty servants, apart from the ostlers in the 100-horse stable. Waiters wore special shoes of goatskin to enable them to walk quietly in the dining room!

Unfortunately the Mail only waited five minutes before crossing the Menai Bridge into Anglesey. Telford's bridge took six years to complete, and on 30th January, 1826, it was opened to the Holyhead Mail:

> At 35 mins past 1 o'clock a.m. the Royal London and Holyhead mail coach conveying the London mail-bags for Dublin to pass: David Davies, Coachman, Wm. Read, Guard. The Mail was followed by the Bangor Pilot, London, Oxford, and Holyhead "Oxonian", the Holyhead Road Commissioners, the Engineer, and several thousand of persons.

With the opening of the bridge the ferry ceased. The rights had been leased by Queen Elizabeth 1 to John William of Conway for £3.6s.8d. per annum, and this could well have been the renewal of an earlier lease.

They heard the case for compensation for the loss of these rights at the Beaumaris Assize, which was finally agreed in 1825 at a figure of £26,394. The ferries were flat-bottomed barges, rowed by four to six men.

The bridge behind them, the coach moved quickly over an exposed road. Here a gentleman could easily lose his top hat unless anchored down by a long neck scarf, which was the method adopted by the more experienced travellers. They knew the Holyhead Mail did not stop for lost "toppers".

The only change while crossing the island was at Caea Mon (Mona Inn).

At five to eleven they arrived at Holyhead. The passengers quickly left the coach and just as quickly were hustled aboard the waiting packet. These passengers although tired and stiff had experienced a reasonable journey at this time of the year, ending with a fair crossing to Ireland. Imagine, however, the journey in winter. Frozen stiff with cold for twenty-seven hours, no sleep and only hurried and inadequate meals, and then to arrive at Holyhead to face a stormy crossing of the Irish Sea. A strong stomach was required in this exercise!

The sirens of the steam packet sounded as they cast off the mooring ropes, and she pulled away from the jetty. Before the packet reached Howth for Dublin the coachman and guard would leave again at a quarter past four with the up Mail for Llangollen and then on to London via Shrewsbury.

Many would agree with De Quincey that the Holyhead was the "grandest of all the Mails". It had to compete in time with the fastest day coaches in the race to Shrewsbury, it had to face and conquer the immense difficulties of the mountain road from Llangollen to Bangor, and it had to cover almost 260 miles, including all stops, in twenty-seven hours with the accuracy of a clock.

The pace was arduous. Hard on the horses and only the best of them could stand the strain. Hard on the coachmen with fifty miles or so of fast driving. Hard on the guards with all their responsibilities throughout the entire journey.

Whatever the weather, whatever the difficulties they encountered, the Mail must get through on time. Everyone knew this. Coachmen, innholders, horse keepers, ostlers and keepers of the turnpike gates, all had to assist the guard in sparing no efforts to see that this was achieved.

The tradition of the service is still remembered by many today.

Glossary

ARTIST	Expert coachman
BENJAMIN	Greatcoat worn by coachmen
BIT OF FISH	Passengers not entered on the Way-bill, or timesheet
BOTH SIDES OF THE ROAD (ALSO TWO SWEATS)	Team worked up and back a stage, the same day
BYE-COACH	Cross-country coach
BYE-MAIL	Cross-country Mail coach
BYE-MAILS	Letter bags sent across country, not via London
COCK-HORSE	Additional horse to assist the team on steep hills. Ridden by a postillion
CROSS-TEAM	Two greys and two darker ones
FEATHER EDGING IT	Driving very close
HANDLING THE RIBBONS	Holding the reins
JOBMASTER	Person who hired out horses, harness and vehicles. Either carried on business at a coach office or at an inn.
KICKING THEM	Asking for a fare
LEADERS	Front pair of a four horse team
LOWER GROUND	Near destination
MAIL BAGS	Sometimes known as letter bags
MAIL COACH	Always referred to as "the Mail"
MAIL RECEIVING OFFICE	Country inn which received letters
MIDDLE GROUND	In between starting point and destination
PUTTEN 'EM TO	Harnessing the team
PYKIE	Keeper of turnpike or toll gate
SCALY ONE	Passenger who gave a small tip
SHOULDERING	Not declaring passengers
SPRINGING THE TEAM	Putting the team into a canter at the bottom of a steep hill
STAGE	Distance between one change of horse and another
STAGECOACH	Public coach running over an advertised route. Almost always named, for example, *Rocket*, *Telegraph* and so on

158

STONES	Cobbles in towns
SUB-OFFICE	Sub-post office
TWO COCK-HORSES	Known as a long set
UP MAIL	Travelling up to London
UPPER GROUND	Near London or other point of departure
WHEELERS	Rear pair of a four horse team